SON OF JOSEPH

SON OF JOSEPH
The Parentage of Jesus

by
Geoffrey Parrinder

T&T CLARK
EDINBURGH

T&T CLARK
59 GEORGE STREET
EDINBURGH EH2 2LQ
SCOTLAND

First published 1992

ISBN 0 567 29213 4

British Library Cataloguing-in-Publication Data

A catalogue record for this book is
available from the British Library

Typeset by Trinity typesetting, Edinburgh.
Printed and bound in Great Britain by Dotesios Ltd, Wiltshire

Contents

Foreword

An account of a Virginal Conception of Jesus is detailed certainly in only one passage of eight verses in the Bible (Matthew 1, 18-25). Few doctrines have had such a slender foundation. The overwhelming evidences of the rest of the New Testament, including other portions of Matthew's Gospel, ignore or refute the notion of supernatural parentage.

Belief in a Virgin Birth, in the sense of the perpetual virginity of Mary, is not mentioned in the Bible, and it appeared only in apocryphal writings from the second century.

Many modern students of the Bible, Christians and others, recognise these facts, but what are the alternatives? Who was regarded as the true father of Jesus? Was Jesus fully human? How large was the family at Nazareth? Are not marriage and sex the gifts of God?

In the second century the critic Celsus suggested, without proof, a passing Roman soldier as the father of Jesus. The poet William Blake imagined that 'Mary was found in Adulterous bed'. In church tradition, with a fear or repudiation of sex, Joseph was pushed into the background and Jesus was presented virtually as the child of a one-parent family.

But the dominant testimony of the Bible is that Joseph, the carpenter, young husband of Mary, was the natural and legitimate father of Jesus. Instead of the later traditional picture of a Holy Family of only two or three, it should include the two parents and their seven or eight children which the Gospels indicate. Joseph, as head of this large family, would have shaped the life and thought of Jesus as much or more than Mary.

This family pattern, with human fatherhood as well as motherhood, has long been ignored or rejected in Christian teaching, though it was believed in by Biblical writers and by early Jewish Christians. Its frank acceptance now may help towards a fuller understanding of incarnation and humanity, of married love and family life.

Is not this Jesus, the son of Joseph,
whose father and mother we know?
John 6, 42

1

His Father's Line

It is a fair guess that in few or no churches in the western world will the first part of the Nativity stories be read at Christmas. The first section, of the first chapter, of the first Gospel, Matthew 1, 1-17 is a genealogy, 'the book of the generation of Jesus Christ'.

This family tree, according to Matthew, traces the ancestry of Jesus from king David and the patriarch Abraham, down to Joseph as his putative father. It states that there were fourteen plus fourteen plus fourteen generations: 'Abraham begat Isaac, and Isaac begat Jacob', and so on. These would add up to forty-two generations in all, symbolical multiples of the sacred number seven. Luke's Gospel (3, 23-38) has a different genealogy, tracing the forebears of Jesus through seventy-seven generations from Joseph to Adam.

To most modern western Christians genealogies may appear tedious, with a succession of 'begats', and so the passages are not studied. The relevance of the family trees may not be clear, their attention to the number seven appears to be artificial, and they are difficult and confusing to read in church services. Further, there are awkward questions, both about the comparison of the lists in the two Gospels and about their contents and reliability.

But to many ancient and eastern or African peoples family trees have been of great interest. In the Islamic world the standard life of Muhammad opens with the genealogy of the Prophet, over five hundred years later than the Bible. His ancestry is traced through fifty generations back to Ishmael and Abraham, finally arriving at Adam.[1]

---

[1]A. Guillaume, *The Life of Muhammad*, translated 1955, p. 3.

1

In the early Christian churches there was clearly much concern with the pedigree of Jesus as the Messiah. This appears in the epistles where Paul writes that Jesus was 'of the seed of David according to the flesh' (Romans 1, 3). And debates are recorded in the Gospels querying of the Christ that 'David himself calls him Lord; so how is he his son?' (Mark 12, 37).

So it is understandable that, for the interest of early Christians, lists of ancestors of Jesus were provided in two Gospels. But it is perplexing that the lists conflict with each other, trace the descent only through the male line, and therefore seem to require that Joseph was his father.

* * * * *

The genealogy provided in the Gospel according to Matthew has several peculiarities: the inclusion of five women, who nevertheless do not count in the succession; an obsession with numbers; and ambiguity over the roles of Joseph and Mary at the end.

'Why bring on the ladies?' queries the Roman Catholic scholar Raymond E. Brown in his massive, critical yet partly conservative study of *The Birth of the Messiah*.[2] The answer might be that four of these women were no ladies, from Matthew's viewpoint. For the five named females are not, as might have been expected in the ancestry of the Messiah, great mothers of the Hebrews like Sarah, Rebecca or Rachel. The five women selected by Matthew for mention are Tamar, Rahab, Ruth, Bath-sheba, and Mary.

It was the Jewish tradition to follow the family succession solely through the male line, and this Matthew does, yet he includes the five women on the way and the reason is uncertain. Various suggestions have been made to explain their presence in Matthew's genealogy, and they do not appear in Luke. Martin Luther considered that the four Old Testament women were regarded as foreigners and they were put in to show that the ancestry of Jesus would interest Gentiles as well as Jews. But only Rahab and Ruth were clearly non-Israelites and even they

[2]R. E. Brown, *The Birth of the Messiah*, 1979 edition, p. 71ff.

were presented in Jewish literature as converts to Judaism. And this theory separated them from Mary who was clearly Jewish.

In the fourth century the patristic writer Jerome with more likelihood suggested that the four women were regarded as sinners, and their inclusion in the list indicated that Jesus was the Saviour of sinners. A modification of this view today agrees that there may have been irregular or scandalous elements in the lives of these four people, but they play vital roles in the ancestry of Christ and so they were instruments of divine providence. But perhaps Matthew's aim was simpler than this, as a consideration of the persons and of Matthew's own text may show.

The first woman named is Tamar who, in Genesis 38, played the harlot to get a son by her father-in-law Judah. She bore him twins and the firstborn Perez passed on the succession to his son. The mention of Tamar in Matthew's list was not necessary for the dynasty, so that she can only be significant in relation to Mary at the end.

'Salmon the father of Boaz by Rahab' says Matthew next. Rahab was the harlot who, in Joshua 2, received the Israelite spies who were sent into Canaan. She was not a Hebrew, but she and her family were saved when Joshua destroyed Jericho. Matthew's assumption that Rahab was the mother of Boaz, the great-grandfather of David, is nowhere stated in the Old Testament and it seems to be a chronological impossibility. But her supposed union with Salmon would be considered irregular since Rahab was a prostitute.

Ruth became the wife of Boaz, but she was a foreigner from Moab and originally of a non-Israelite religion. Moreover Ruth slept with Boaz before their marriage, 'she came softly, and uncovered his feet, and lay down' (Ruth 3, 7). Such a way of inveigling Boaz into lawful wedlock might cause comment, and it might also provide a comparison with Mary.

'The wife of Uriah', whom Matthew does not name, was Bath-sheba, and her adulterous union with David and his despatch of her husband to death, which brought condemnation from the prophet Nathan, were notorious (2 Samuel 11-12). Bath-sheba bore Solomon to David, but it may be noted that Luke omits Solomon from his list of the forebears of Jesus.

Why were these four women singled out by Matthew, and other more virtuous ladies ignored? Surely the wives of patriarchs, even Hagar or Leah, could have been shown as more worthy than these women? It has been suggested that Matthew selects these four sinful women in an apologetic device to rebut the criticism that Mary also was an adulteress who conceived Jesus in a sinful or irregular relationship. R. E. Brown rejects this view, saying that the women were not all sinners, or if they were they came later to be esteemed as proselytes and models of faith. So he concludes that there is little likelihood that Matthew's readers would have understood the women to have been sinners.[3]

But that is precisely what they were, and it seems probable that was why they were adopted by Matthew, and other women were omitted. The clue must lie at the end of the list, in Mary, or rather in statements made about her. What is she doing in this company?

Following the genealogy Matthew (1, 18-25) asserts that Mary had been betrothed to Joseph, but 'before they came together she was found to be with child'. Joseph, 'being a just man and unwilling to put her to shame, resolved to divorce her quietly'. But then he was told by an angel in a dream that the conception was of 'a holy spirit'. With Mary, as with the four named Old Testament women in the genealogy, there were thought to be irregular or wrongful circumstances in the production of offspring (in Matthew, but probably not in Luke, see later).

To defend Mary's reputation, or support his belief in a virginal conception, Matthew selected four Old Testament women to show that despite marital irregularities or open scandal they could fit into the providential scheme. So Mary's virtue was proved, or her condition was justifiable, though this was a rather ham-fisted way of showing it.

The choice of these women for the genealogy in Matthew can be related to his purposes in writing the infancy narratives. But the genealogy and the virginal conception are not referred to in the succeeding birth stories, they find no mention in the

[3] *ibid.*, p. 72.

rest of the Gospel, and they are separate from Matthew's theology in general. The genealogy and the adjacent tales belong to a different, and probably later, stage than the bulk of the Gospel. They would come from Matthew's own writing or editing, or from his circle, rather than from the pre-Matthean material which he used for accounts of the life and teaching of Jesus.

As the other women were not relevant for the Davidic or Abrahamic succession, neither was Mary. After all that, the genealogy would only be significant if Joseph was the true father, as will be seen.

* * * * *

'Could Matthew count?' asks R. E. Brown,[4] for although Matthew claims that his list gives three times fourteen generations, the names do not add up, the arithmetic leaves something to be desired. The first section from Abraham to David provides fourteen names but only thirteen begettings or generations. From David to the Babylonian Exile fourteen generations are given, but in the last section from the Exile to Jesus again there are only thirteen generations.

Various attempts have been made to solve these omissions or inconsistencies: some wicked kings may have been omitted, but even more wicked ones like Manasseh are included. Names of kings such as Jehoiakim and Jehoiachin (Jechoniah) may have been confused. Jesus may have been the thirteenth generation in the last section, and the Christ the fourteenth. But Matthew holds that Jesus was Christ from the beginning.

Comparing Matthew's genealogical list with Luke's the latter seems more plausible, but it is hardly exact. Luke (3, 23-38) traces the ancestry of Jesus beyond Abraham, perhaps to broaden the interest beyond Israel for the Gentile churches. There is also a possible reference to the Pauline teaching of Jesus as the second Adam. Luke's ending with 'Adam, son of God' is astonishing and without parallel in Jewish tradition. For, as C. F. Evans remarks, Adam was not son of God 'in the

[4] *ibid.* p. 81ff.

same physical sense in which others in his list were sons of their fathers'. It is either a simple statement of the divine activity in creation, or it ends the genealogy to tie up with the verse before the beginning, in which Jesus had been declared to be the beloved Son of God.[5]

Luke does not claim that his genealogy follows a numerical system, as Matthew does, but he lists seven patriarchs from Adam to Enoch, and seventy names between Enoch and Jesus. Again the name Jesus appears in the forty-ninth place, in a namesake of Jesus. And Luke gives twenty-one names in the post-exilic period as against Matthew's fourteen. Some commentators have indicated the influence of a late apocryphal Book of Enoch, which claimed seventy-seven generations from Adam to the Last Judgment.[6] But there are variations in the manuscripts of Luke which give figures ranging from seventy-seven to sixty-three.[7]

Any student of these two Gospel genealogies may be struck by a major difference close to the end (or the beginning). Who was Jesus's grandfather? According to Matthew his name was Jacob, but in Luke it is given as Heli or Eli. This problem has puzzled writers for a long time, and the fourth century church historian Eusebius quotes the third century Julius Africanus who claimed that Jacob and Eli were half-brothers and when Eli died without children Jacob married his widow in a Levirate marriage which produced Joseph. Most modern commentators think this explanation too good to be true, though some suggest that it might come from a family tradition. The general conclusion seems to be that the genealogies tell us nothing certain about the grand-parents of Jesus. Matthew and Luke both have the more theological concern to show that Jesus was son of David, and son of Abraham, and son of Adam, and son of God.[8]

[5]C. F. Evans, *Saint Luke*, 1990, p. 253.

[6]R. Bauckham, *Jude and the Relatives of Jesus in the Early Church*, 1990, p. 318ff.

[7]R. E. Brown, op. cit., p. 91, note 74.

[8]*ibid.*, p. 94; Eusebius, *The History of the Church*, translated by G. A. Williamson, 1965, 1, 7, 4; p. 53ff.

Where did these genealogical tables come from? Partly from the post-exilic book of Chronicles which opens with nine chapters of genealogy, and there were later lineages composed of the tribes of Levi and Judah and the house of David. It has been suggested that Matthew used an existing Davidic genealogy, and different families may have claimed royal lineage without all being in direct succession, varying lists circulating in different circles. Matthew and Luke, or their sources, added at least the names of Joseph and Jesus, but whether their family was in direct or lateral succession from David may be questioned, and this will be considered later (see on Son of David).

The differences between the lists in Matthew and Luke have been explained by suggesting that Matthew used Joseph's records and Luke used Mary's. But there is no evidence for such a hypothesis, and it is untenable because the genealogies are both traced through the fathers and not the mothers. Moreover Luke insists as strongly as Matthew that Joseph was of the house and lineage of David, and there is no proof that Mary was of Davidic descent. If she was a kinswoman of Elizabeth she would be a Levite (Luke 1, 5 and 36).

It may be that Matthew's genealogy follows a popular local Christian tradition about Davidic lineage, adding the names of Joseph and Jesus. Luke in a different place may give a family list of Joseph's ancestors, linking them to another tradition. The brothers of Jesus may have claimed Davidic ancestry, and this will be discussed later.[9]

The genealogies may be taken as symbolical and theological, rather than strictly historical. They aim at showing that the people of God are children of Abraham, and the Messiah is the son of David. Yet while the formulation of the genealogies seems to have been both devout and tortuous, it could be regarded as unnecessary. If Jesus was the Messiah for faith he would be considered to be son of David by right, as suggested elsewhere in the Gospels, 'the Christ is son of David' (Mark 12, 35, and parallels). There is no sign of anyone deducing either that Jesus was Messiah because he was a son of David, or opposing the Messianic claim by questioning his Davidic descent.

* * * * *

[9]Bauckham, op. cit., p. 358f.

The Roman Catholic scholar Hans Küng writes that the contradictions between the genealogies given in Matthew and Luke 'cannot be harmonized', but he notes that they both come down to 'Joseph (not to Mary!)', his exclamation mark.[10]

Matthew's genealogy is not only peculiar in that it includes five women, who yet do not count in the succession, and that it has an obsession with numbers that do not add up or fully correspond to Luke's or to Old Testament lists; there is also ambiguity over the roles of Joseph and Mary at the end.

Matthew 1, 16 reads: 'Jacob begot Joseph, the husband of Mary, of whom was begotten [or born] Jesus, who is called Christ.' This is the reading of the major manuscripts. However, there are two other readings with some textual support.

Some modern translations give as a footnote that 'Other ancient authorities read, "Joseph, to whom was betrothed the virgin Mary, begot Jesus," or "was the father of Jesus".' The principal support for this is the Old Syriac version. Another variant, from minor Greek and Latin versions, reads, 'Joseph, to whom the betrothed virgin Mary bore Jesus'.

It would have been natural, and in accordance with the invariable pattern of the genealogy in following the male line, for the list to have ended by simply saying that 'Jacob begot Joseph and he begot Jesus'. The strongest text may still imply that Joseph was the father of Jesus, with an imperfect adjustment to the following narrative of a virginal conception, since it uses the passive 'was begotten' instead of the active 'begot'.

Commentators have discussed these variants at length, some thinking it incredible that Matthew wrote 'Joseph begot Jesus', when he went on straight away to assert the virginal conception in 1, 18-25. But it is probable that Matthew was using different traditions for the separate stories of the Nativity that are gathered together in his first two chapters. There are awkward links between these various narratives, as well as many differences from Luke's Nativity tales.

A further possibility is that one of the above readings was original, and stated that Joseph was the biological father of

---

[10]H. Küng, *On Being a Christian*, English translation 1978, p. 451.

Jesus, but that later copyists changed the text under the growing insistence in the church on the perpetual virginity of Mary. It is also possible that there was an early version of Matthew in circulation which did not include the first two chapters. Further, there were known to be some Christians, especially Jewish, who taught positively that Joseph was the father of Jesus (see Chapter 10 below). The current Gospel of Matthew does speak later of Jesus as 'the carpenter's son' (13, 55), and this also will be considered in due course.

Like Matthew, Luke has an ambiguous phrase to link his genealogy with the different narratives of the conception and birth of Jesus. Luke 3, 23 reads: 'Jesus, being the son (as was supposed) of Joseph, the son of Heli.' Some commentators regard the phrase 'as was supposed' to be a 'redactional addition to the genealogy', or 'an addition to cover a discrepancy'.[11] Either Luke himself, or a redactor, attempts to reconcile the genealogy, which had to be traced through Joseph, with a virginal conception which seemed to exclude Joseph. But, as a Jewish authority asks, if the supposition of Joseph's parentage was erroneous 'why did Luke, and the tradition responsible for the genealogical table before him, waste their time compiling a sequence of irrelevant ancestors?'[12]

Whether Luke's earlier narrative of the annunciation to Mary clearly indicates belief in a virginal conception or not, and this will be discussed later, that belief is stated plainly in Matthew, after the genealogical table. Luke may have had Matthew's Gospel before him, or the belief may have been in circulation elsewhere.

It should be repeated in connection with the genealogical tables, that if Joseph was not the father of Jesus there would have been no point in compiling them. The circles in which they were put together probably considered Joseph to be the natural and legitimate father, but the lists were later fitted on to quite separate narratives.

The importance of the genealogies for readers today is not merely that they claim ancestry from David or Abraham for Jesus, but that in both Matthew and Luke the lists suggest that Jesus was regarded as the son of Joseph in the early church communities in which they were compiled.

[11]Bauckham p. 369; J. M. Creed, *The Gospel According to St Luke*, 1930, p. 59.
[12]G. Vermes, *Jesus the Jew*, 1983 edition, p. 215.

2

Annunciation and Nativity — Matthew

The Annunciation and Nativity stories of Matthew 1-2 read like folk tales, with five messages in dreams and five claimed fulfilments of prophecy. Hans Küng says of these and of Luke's narratives that 'today of course it is admitted even by Catholic exegetes that these stories are a collection of largely uncertain, mutually contradictory, and strongly legendary and ultimately theologically motivated narratives, with a character of their own'.[1]

The Anglican Professor John Macquarrie also puts it forcibly: 'the stories of apparitions of angels or of the star that led the wise men to Bethlehem, however much they have come to be loved in Christian tradition, have no historical value, and I suspect, very little theological value either . . . they try to enhance the significance of Christ by introducing supernatural prodigies'.[2]

The infancy tales are not properly history, though some historical persons may appear. But the narratives are the product of early Christian meditation and speculation, seeking to fit in with various Biblical words, and emphasising the Messiahship of Jesus from the very beginning. They are faith-history, and if the stories are taken in this way some of the contradictions and improbabilities may seem to be resolved, or they may be ignored as they have done down the ages in Nativity plays.

Yet the modern historical sense requires examination of the narratives, and for theology it may be that critical study can

---

[1] *On Being a Christian*, p. 451.
[2] J. Macquarrie, *Jesus Christ in Modern Thought*, 1990, p. 393.

reveal a more satisfying picture than hitherto of the humanity
of Jesus and the values of family life.

* * * * *

The first two chapters of Matthew, and parallels in Luke, are
separate from the rest of the Gospel records and they are never
referred to again in accounts of the life of Jesus, nor in claims
made for him, nor in disputes about his office and nature.
There is no indication that Jesus ever spoke of the circumstances
of his birth, and his mother seems to have been surprised when
he became famous (Matthew 12, 46, etc.).

After Matthew's genealogical table, tracing a family line
from Abraham to Joseph and Jesus, there follow eight verses
which are the clearest and perhaps the only statements of belief
in a virginal conception in the whole of the New Testament.

When Mary is 'found' to be pregnant by 'holy spirit', an
angel reassures Joseph in a dream saying: 'Joseph, son of David,
do not fear to take Mary your wife, for that which is conceived
in her is of holy spirit.' There are no definite articles or capital
letters in the original Greek here, or in the parallel passages in
Luke, though modern translations tend to provide both. Yet
early English Protestant Bibles used capitals for neither 'holy'
nor 'spirit' nor 'ghost', and the Authorised (King James)
Version used capitals only for 'Spirit' until the eighteenth
century.

This is more than a matter of style, for to translate *the Holy
Spirit* might suggest that this is the third Person of the Trinity,
a male element in the union with Mary. But the Trinitarian
theology had not been developed, and the use of the term
'spirit', as commentators have noted, was 'the broader category
of divine agent', the 'force by which God moved the prophets
to speak' and which descended on Jesus at his baptism.[3]

The story is artificial, for Mary is 'found' to be with child, as
if she did not know and Joseph or others spotted her condition.
According to Luke Mary had received the announcement
three months or more earlier. Were there two independent

[3] R. E. Brown, *The Birth of the Messiah*, p. 125.

annunciations?' 'As a wag has remarked, that theory presupposes
that Mary and Joseph never spoke to each other.'[4] This is a
further sign that Matthew's and Luke's narratives are
independent of each other, are often contradictory, and can
hardly be reconciled.

* * * * *

Matthew has a remarkable way of regarding events as happening
in order to fulfil some prophecy, and before the development
of the modern critical study of scripture it was taken for granted
by commentators that the Old Testament prophets were
foretelling the future. It was assumed that God had indicated
the Christian scheme of salvation, even the Virgin Birth, in the
Hebrew Bible. Not only liberals but fairly conservative writers
now agree that 'this conception of prophecy as prediction of
the distant future has disappeared from most serious scholarship
today, and it is widely recognised that the NT "fulfilment" of the
OT involved much that the OT writers did not foresee at all.
The OT prophets were primarily concerned with addressing
God's challenge to their own times'.[5]

Yet Matthew continued that 'all of this took place to fulfil
what the Lord had spoken by the prophet: Behold, the virgin
shall conceive and bear a son, and his name shall be called
Emmanuel, which means, God with us'. It is astonishing that
Matthew baldly asserts that the virginal conception happened
in order to fulfil a prophecy, and not the other way round. Most
theologians would not accept such an interpretation. It should
be noted that ancient and modern translators into English
have tended to render the words 'a virgin', but both the Greek
and the Hebrew use the definite article, 'the virgin' or 'the
young woman'.

The prophetic reference is to Isaiah 7, and both the
circumstances and the words of that chapter need brief
consideration if the correct sense is to be understood. About
740 B.C. the rulers of Syria and northern Israel marched

[4]*ibid.*, p. 525.
[5]*ibid.*, p. 146.

against Jerusalem and struck terror into its king Ahaz and his people. The prophet Isaiah went to tell Ahaz that his enemies were only fag-ends of firebrands and would soon go out. Ahaz should ask for a sign from God, but he piously replied that he would not tempt the Lord.

Thereupon Isaiah declared that God himself would provide a sign: 'The young woman shall conceive and bear a son, and shall call his name Immanuel', to show her faith that God is with them. And before the child knows how to distinguish between good and harmful foods, the two enemy kingdoms will be destroyed. This event happened shortly afterwards.

Yet the sign given by Isaiah was not centred on the manner in which the child would be conceived, but on its timing to show the presence of God with his people in their distress. An ancient Jewish interpretation identified this child with Hezekiah, who was son and successor to Ahaz and one of the most devout kings of Judah.

Modern exposition has centred on the meaning of the word translated 'virgin' or 'young woman'. The Hebrew word used in Isaiah 7, 14 was *'almā*, which normally indicated a young girl at the age of puberty and therefore marriageable. The Revised Standard Version translates this word as 'young woman', with footnote 'Or virgin'.

The presence of the definite article, '*the* young woman', suggests that Isaiah may have been referring to someone known, perhaps a recent young wife in the king's harem or, as suggested above, the mother of Hezekiah.

But Matthew uses the Greek Septuagint translation of Isaiah where the word given is *parthenos*, which is more usually 'virgin', though there are exceptions to this usage. Matthew has already stated that Mary was pregnant before she came together with Joseph. Eager to find support from the scriptures, which seemed to imply that a divine impregnation had been predicted, Matthew forces the word and the sense from Isaiah, as well as ignoring completely the historical context of Isaiah's statements. It is far from the last of his artificial applications of scriptures to dogmatic purposes.

Not all early Christians, especially some Jewish Christians, accepted the notion of a virginal conception (see later on Early

Humanism, chapter 10), and it was also part of debates between other Christians and orthodox Jews. The early Christian philosopher Justin Martyr in the mid-second century wrote a *Dialogue with Trypho*, representing Jewish criticism of Matthew's interpretation of the Old Testament.

The Jewish Trypho is reported as saying, 'The scripture has not, Behold the virgin [parthenos] shall conceive and bear a son, but Behold the young woman [neanis] shall conceive and bear a son, and the rest of it as you say. But the whole prophecy was spoken of Hezekiah, and in him it is proved that the things were fulfilled according to this prophecy'.[6]

Trypho, according to Justin, traced the idea of a virginal conception to Greek rather than Hebrew influence, and he said that 'you ought to be ashamed of telling the same tale as they . . . lest you be convicted of making fools of yourselves like the Greeks'.

Later in the second century the anti-Christian writing of Celsus asserted that Mary was driven out by her carpenter-husband because she had committed adultery with a soldier named Panthera, either a name invented for a supposed father of Jesus or a garbled version of *parthenos*.

In orthodox Judaism the ideas of virginal conception or divine impregnation were unknown, and the nearest approach would be in legends of heroes like Isaac or Samuel. Sarah had passed the menopause (Genesis 18, 11) and Abraham was said to be a hundred years old, yet God gave them a son, Isaac. Hannah was barren, but in response to her prayers and vows God gave her a son, Samuel. But there is no suggestion in either story that the fathers had no part in the conceptions. On the contrary, God opened the women's wombs, and both female sterility and male impotence were changed by divine power. The Old Testament parallel is more with the story in Luke of the child John given to the aged Zechariah and barren Elizabeth.

Whatever Greek influence there may have been on Matthew or his circle, his brief statement of a virginal conception is in a thoroughly Jewish setting. Prophecy is quoted in support of his claim, even if it is misinterpreted; though if there was no

[6]*Dialogue with Trypho*, 67.

'virgin' in Isaiah then there is no fulfilment of prophecy. The
Jewish Trypho, said Justin, declared that Christians should not
follow the Greeks but 'rather say that this Jesus was a man born
of men, and, if you prove from the Scriptures that he is the
Christ, that he was counted worthy of being chosen for the
Christ because he lived a perfect life and according to the law'.

* * * * *

Matthew ends this section by stating that Joseph 'knew her not',
or 'had no sexual relations' with Mary, until she had borne her
son, Jesus. This seems to imply that they did have sexual
relations afterwards, and the Gospels later name brothers and
sisters of Jesus. But this sexual relationship has been fiercely
disputed by those who hold to a belief in the perpetual virginity
of Mary, a belief but not a dogma, which has divided Christians.
R. E. Brown confesses that 'in my judgment the question of
Mary's remaining a virgin for the rest of her life belongs to post-
biblical theology'.[7] In later apocryphal and monastic writings,
when celibacy was praised above marriage, there emerged
notions that Mary had taken a vow of lifelong virginity, and that
her marriage with Joseph was simply a matter of convenience
(see chapter 11 below).

The biblical evidence is strongly against such world-
renouncing and sex-denying theories. They are quite
unHebraic, as Brown says again, 'quite unlikely on the
Palestinian scene'.[8] Not only does Matthew 1, 25 imply later
sexual relations, but Luke 2, 7 writes of Jesus as Mary's 'firstborn son'. Further, there are the facts of the brothers and
sisters of Jesus, of whom there is no textual reason to doubt as
the further children of Joseph and Mary: 'Is not this the
carpenter's son? Is not his mother called Mary? And are not his
brothers James and Joseph and Simon and Judas? And are not
all his sisters with us?' (Matthew 13, 55; Mark 6, 3; see also other
references to his brothers and sisters, and chapter 5 below).

[7] *The Birth of the Messiah*, p. 132.
[8] *ibid.*, p. 306.

There is no suggestion in any of these biblical references of a perpetual virginity of Mary, but rather the opposite. The continued motherhood of Mary, and fatherhood of Joseph, the richness of family life given and blessed by God, these are the pictures provided by the New Testament in patterns of both holy and normal living.

* * * * *

The rest of Matthew's infancy narratives may be mentioned briefly. In a continued search for prophecies Matthew seems to have used a collection of 'testimonies', Old Testament verses that early Christians collected when they were thought to be applicable to Christ, since full biblical manuscripts were not easily available in either Hebrew or Greek. So odd verses are quoted to support the legends of sensational happenings: the visit of the Magi, the birth in Bethlehem, massacre of the innocents, flight into Egypt, and final settlement at Nazareth. These extraordinary events are not attested in any secular source, and it is remarkable that Luke also does not refer to most of them, and he contradicts some openly or by implication.

According to Luke, Joseph and Mary lived in Nazareth already, and they went for the birth 'from Galilee, from the town of Nazareth . . . to Bethlehem, because Joseph was of the house and lineage of David'. But in Matthew it seems that the couple are thought to live in Bethlehem, in a 'house' where the Magi visit them, rather than the stable or common room where Luke situates the birth. Matthew then sees the young family going to Nazareth only after returning from Egypt, since they leave their home in Judea and go up to Galilee for fear of Archelaus who reigns in Judea in place of Herod.

From his testimonies Matthew finds support for the birth of Jesus in Bethlehem. In Micah 5, 2 it was said that from Bethlehem would 'come forth for me one who is to be ruler in Israel'. This may originally have meant that the promised ruler would come from the family of David who originated from Bethlehem. It is one of several prophecies of a promised one in descent from David, but Matthew pins it on to Bethlehem town. R. E. Brown admits that the evidence 'for birth at Bethlehem is much

weaker than the evidence for Davidic descent'.[9] But the problem
of Bethlehem is aside from our present purpose, which is to
discover and affirm the paternity of Joseph and the full family
life at Nazareth.

Matthew's notion of a guiding star for the wise men to
indicate a promised ruler may have been derived from Numbers
24, 17: 'A star shall come forth out of Jacob, and a sceptre shall
rise out of Israel.' The Magi bring gifts, as in Isaiah 60: 'nations
shall come to your light, and kings . . . they shall bring gold and
incense'. 'Myrrh and frankincense' are noted as coming from
the wilderness, in Song of Songs 3, 6.

The wise men from the east are Magi (*magoi*), not 'astrologers'
as in some modern translations, but priests of the Zoroastrian
religion of Persia. They represent the Gentiles coming to pay
tribute to the king 'of the Jews'. The narrative of their visit has
been described as 'iconic', a story in the scriptures 'which
critical historians reject as accounts of objective facts'.[10] Yet
whatever the value of the details in Matthew's narrative may be,
it is an interesting recognition of Zoroastrian influence upon
Judeo-Christian religion. The Magi did spread some of their
religious perceptions into the Semitic world. Cyrus the Persian
was hailed as the Lord's anointed in Isaiah 45, and he permitted
the return of the Jews from exile in Mesopotamia. Through
Persian influence in the inter-testamental period and in the
New Testament there were developed among the Jews notions
of angels and demons, death and judgment, heaven and hell.
The presence, 'so generally disregarded, of the Iranian religion
in the Judaeo-Christian world', is revealed in a dramatic flash
in the legend of the Magi.[11]

The text does not state that there were three Magi, but this came
to be assumed later from the three gifts and, from Isaiah, that they
were kings. They were not named until Latin legends from the
sixth century, when they were called Gaspar, Melchior and
Balthasar, and given different colours and dress. Later still they
became saints, and their relics are said to be in Cologne cathedral.

[9] *ibid.*, p. 516.

[10] W. M. Watt. *Islamic Fundamentalism and Modernity*, 1988, p. 81.

[11] M. Boyce, *Zoroastrianism: A Shadowy but Powerful Presence in the Judaeo-Christian World*, 1987, p. 18.

The Magi were warned in a dream to go home another way, and after a further dream Joseph and family were sent off to Egypt by an angel. The stories of the massacre of the innocents, and the flight into Egypt, are contradicted by Luke (2, 22 and 39) which says that Joseph and Mary went to Jerusalem to perform everything according to the law and then 'they returned into Galilee, to their own town, Nazareth'.

Matthew supports the legend of the infant massacre by a reference to Jeremiah 31, 15. 'Rachel weeping for her children' first referred to the Jews going into exile in Mesopotamia in the sixth century B.C., passing Rama and Rachel's tomb nearby. Matthew says 'all the boys' were killed, but there is no mention of this in secular histories, such as that of Josephus. Sadly, however, there were many massacres of adults and children in those violent days, and Herod was notorious for his cruelty, instructing his soldiers to kill notable political prisoners if news came of his death.[12]

Further quotations from the prophets were cited to support other stories. 'Out of Egypt I have called my son' came from Hosea 11, 1, where it originally referred to the deliverance of the Israelites from Egypt at the Exodus. National tragedies and triumphs are woven into the story of the infant Messiah, and they have entered into Christian and Islamic legend. In Egypt today there are six sites where the Holy Family is said to have rested. And in the Qur'ān, in the chapter of Mary (19, 22ff.), she shelters under a palm tree and the infant Jesus tells his mother to shake the tree to get the dates, and then he shows her a stream where they can quench their thirst.

On return from Egypt to home in Judea, Joseph's choice of distant Nazareth is justified by Matthew from 'the prophets', saying that 'he shall be called a Nazarene'. There is no direct source for this claim, but commentators have suggested a parallel in the story of Samson in Judges 13, 5, where it is said that 'the boy shall be a Nazirite to God,' an ascetic. The book of Judges was one of the Former Prophets in the Hebrew canon of scripture. Of course Jesus came to be known as a Nazarene

---

[12]For a comparison of Rachel with Mary, see J. Neusner, *Jews and Christians*, 1991, p. 122ff.

from the place of his home, and he was regarded as holy though definitely not an ascetic.

The emphasis upon prophecy in Matthew's stories suggests analogies between those of Moses and Israel and that of Christ. Israel was called God's Son, and Christ as his Son is seen to be fulfilling promises made to Moses and the prophets. The Magi provided a wider dimension, of godly Gentiles coming to revere the promised ruler at Jerusalem and Bethlehem. But endless references in Christian churches to the 'prophecies' each year at Christmas may too easily assume that the Jews were blind and deaf because they could not accept the Messiah so apparently clearly foretold in their own scriptures. This can provide grounds for antisemitism, and therefore these references, and the tales in which they are set, need to be weighed and used carefully and critically.[13]

* * * * *

Finally, for the moment on Matthew, it is important to note that the idea of a virginal conception stated by him in no way suggests that normal procreation would be tainted, either by the carnal nature of sexual intercourse or as a carrier of Original Sin. There is no hint, in either Old or New Testaments, that such defilement needed to be excluded from the nature of Jesus by supernatural procreation.

On this point the doctrine of the Virginal Conception of Jesus is quite different from the much later dogma of the Immaculate Conception of the Virgin Mary, which was promulgated, for the Roman Catholic church only, as late as 1854. It declared that the Virgin Mary was, in the first instant of her conception, 'preserved untouched by any taint of original guilt'. This is a Western, Latin Christian, and quite unscriptural notion.

The Bible does not teach the transmission of a taint of original guilt, and there is no suggestion of its avoidance in the infancy stories of Matthew and Luke, or anywhere else in the New Testament. Even in Matthew's statement that that which

[13]J. Bowden, *Jesus: The Unanswered Questions* 1988, p. 13.

was conceived in Mary was of 'a holy spirit' there is no suggestion of blocking any taint from Joseph. Matthew envisages a positive supernatural power, not a negative blockage. It was Augustine of Hippo in the fifth century who virtually equated Original Sin with sexual emotion, so that every act of coitus was intrinsically evil and children were conceived by the 'sin' of their parents. Augustine was reacting against his own immoral youth, but he had such a great influence on western thought in the succeeding centuries that a modern writer can describe him as the 'corrupter of Christian morals'.[14]

Further, in the development of Christology stress has sometimes been laid upon the Virginal Conception as a guarantee of the 'sinlessness' of Jesus. But again there is no biblical evidence for such a claim. As John Macquarrie says, 'the assertion of Jesus' sinlessness does not depend on any doctrine of virginal conception . . . If one rejects this Augustinian idea of the transmission of original sin, then the need for any break in the heredity of Jesus is seen to be uncalled for. It would in any case compromise his genuine humanity'. And again, 'Equally one must reject another Augustinian idea, that Christ *could not* sin. This again would appear to infringe his true humanity'.[15]

In their fairly conservative commentary on Matthew, Davies and Allison remark that 'affirmation of the virgin birth entangles one in difficult dilemmas. Hence if the traditional belief be maintained, it will have to be on the basis of strictly theological considerations; historical reasoning offers little support'.[16]

In Matthew's story, whether it was fanciful or not, at most the Virginal Conception was regarded as a free act of the power of God. It was comparable to the divine action in the stories of Sarah and Hannah and others, even if with fuller emphasis. But sex was good, given by God. After the birth of Jesus, as firstborn, it is assumed that Joseph 'knew' Mary sexually and they had a large family.

---

[14]Karl Holl, and see J. Burnaby, article 'Augustine of Hippo' in *A Dictionary of Christian Ethics*, 1967, p. 23.

[15]Macquarrie, op. cit., p. 396f.

[16]W. D. Davies and D. C. Allison, *The Gospel according to Saint Matthew*, 1988, p. 216.

The role of Joseph as head of this family is clear in Matthew 2 and 13, 55, in addition to what had gone before. He is depicted as a dreamer, like his namesake the patriarch Joseph in Genesis, but he was also practical. Angels and messages are said to have come to him, giving directions in a series of crises. Joseph was as active here as in the different narratives in Luke, where he took Mary and their son to Bethlehem and back again to Nazareth.

Note on Virginal Conceptions

The Jewish critic Trypho, according to Justin Martyr, having rebutted the notion that a virginal conception had been prophesied by Isaiah, suggested that it came from Gentile influence: 'In the legends of those who are called Greeks we read that Perseus was born of Danae, who was a virgin, and on whom he who is by them called Zeus came down in a shower of gold'.[1]

Trypho might have gone farther and found other myths of virginal conceptions in ancient Egyptian, Greek and Roman mythology. These supposed parallels with the Gospels suggest 'heavenly marriages', or at least coupling of divine and human. The celestial Zeus was particularly active in this manner not only with Danae but with many other women, such as Io, Leda, Semele and Persephone. The abduction of Europa by Zeus in the form of a bull is still to be seen portrayed in a Roman mosaic preserved at Lullingstone in Kent. Great historical characters like Alexander, Augustus and even Plato, were credited with a divine parent, to name but a few. Although there was varying detail in the myths, sexual intercourse of a god with a human woman was usually assumed.[2]

In modern times, with greater knowledge of or easier comparisons with farther Asian religions, more virginal conceptions have been adduced: for example, in myths of Zoroaster, the Buddha and Krishna. Zoroaster might be the most interesting, given the visit of the Persian Magi in Matthew's story. But although in late Zoroastrianism there appeared a belief in a coming Saviour, the Saoshyant, born of a virgin, this would not be Zoroaster himself but one born of the prophet's

[1]*Dialogue with Trypho*, 67.
[2]R. E. Brown, *The Birth of the Messiah*, pp. 517-531.

22

own seed, which had been miraculously preserved in a lake, and when a virgin bathed there she would become pregnant by the prophet. The contrast with Matthew's account could hardly be greater, and the myth is of late appearance.[3]

The legends of the Buddha show gradual development. In the early and probably pre-Christian tales of the Theravada (Hinayana) schools it was written of the Buddha-to-be that 'his father is the rajah Suddhodana, whose wife Maya is his mother'. But in later Mahavastu texts Maya, now a queen, 'a woman like the consort of an immortal', although married went away from her husband, renounced sensual desires, and then the Buddha came down from heaven and entered her womb in the form of a noble white elephant.[4]

The birth of Krishna also had elaborate mythology. The Hindu god Vishnu plucked out two of his own hairs, one white and the other black, the black becoming the dark Krishna in the womb of Devaki the wife of Vasudeva. The Hindu avatars (often taken as 'incarnations') are multiple, and even in the austere Bhagavad Gita the god Krishna says that he generates himself age after age.[5]

The farther mythologies of Asia, or the nearer ones of Greece and Rome, seem distinct from the biblical world and outside influences appear the more unlikely as they are studied. Whether Gentile or Hellenized Jewish Christians would have found the pagan myths acceptable is improbable. The gross sexual activities of Zeus would undoubtedly have been repulsive.

There is no suggestion in the Bible of a 'heavenly marriage' or any hint of a divine coupling or penetration. Matthew says that 'that which is conceived in her is of holy spirit', the divine power which was seen to be the fulfilment of a prophecy. Although there is no reason to believe that Isaiah 7, 14 originally indicated a virginal conception, or that it was interpreted in

[3]M. Boyce, *Zoroastrians*, 1979, p. 42.

[4]*Mahapadana Suttanta* 30; *Mahavastu* 2, 2. See G. Parrinder, *Sex in the World's Religions*, 1980, p. 41f.

[5]*Vishnu Purana* 5, 2; *Bhagavad Gita* 4, 6-8. See G. Parrinder, *Avatar and Incarnation*, 1970, p. 19ff. On other virginal conceptions, see also M. Warner, *Alone of all her Sex*, 1976, chapter 3.

this way by orthodox Jews, Matthew has taken this passage to indicate such a belief.[6]

It used to be assumed that Matthew's story of the annunciation must have come from Joseph himself, or from relatives or friends to whom he had told it. But there is no evidence whatever for this supposition. On the contrary, the silence of all Christian writings before Matthew regarding virginal conception is strongly against the notion. Critical study suggests much greater likelihood that Matthew, or his circle, composed the narrative to fit in with interpretation of prophecy. Searching the scriptures for any possible references to the Messiah they came to Isaiah 7, 14. The Christ was certainly believed to be Immanuel, God with us. But the Greek *parthenos* was taken to indicate a virgin in the prophecy and so a virginal conception was assumed. A pious tale, like part of a historical novel, would be composed to give setting and detail, and the child's undoubted name Jesus was evidence that he would save his people from their sins. This was not factual history, or even Greek myth, but a form of popular Jewish interpretation of scripture, Midrash, which recent writers say 'may be terse or discursive, straightforward or fanciful, and more or less amply spiced with analogies, parables and legends'.[7]

If the story of the virginal conception had been derived from or influenced by Greek myths of divine coupling with a human female, then those feminists would be right who have seen in it a demeaning of woman. Christ would be fathered by God, his divinity coming from his heavenly father and his physical body from his passive human mother. By extension men could be regarded as spiritual and women as physical and submissive.

But, as we have noted before in remarking on *a* holy spirit, rather than *the* Holy Spirit, there is no masculinity involved. Moreover, 'spirit' is female in Hebrew and neuter in Greek. Matthew was a Jew, and his tradition honoured marriage and the procreative process, and it is fair to say that he could not foresee all that might result from his story with the later

---

[6]*The Birth of the Messiah*, p. 524.

[7]D. J. Goldberg and J. D. Rayner, *The Jewish People*, 1987, p. 212, also W. D. Davies and D. C. Allison, op. cit., p. 195.

church's emphasis on celibacy and priestly aversion to women and sexual contacts. In fact, in his story it is Joseph who suffers, by being eliminated from the process of conception, although the previous genealogical table required the full participation of Joseph in passing on the succession from David and Abraham.

3

Annunciation and Nativity — Luke

In studying the accounts of the birth of Jesus it is essential to recognise the independence from one another of the two Gospels, Matthew and Luke, which contain the infancy tales, and their differences from each other.

From the early centuries there have been tendencies to draw together the records of these two Gospels, especially in popular nativity plays but also in ordinary exposition. But this was a mistake, according to R. E. Brown: 'Throughout I have insisted that the two stories are very different, that neither evangelist knew the other's work, and that efforts at harmonizing the narratives into one consecutive story are quite impossible'.[1]

Like Matthew the third Gospel relates narratives of events surrounding the birth of Jesus, which are never referred to again in the accounts of his ministry. In his formal prefatory verses Luke says that 'Many have undertaken to compile a narrative of these things', as they were delivered by 'those who from the beginning were eyewitnesses'. Despite this 'it seemed good to me also, having followed all things closely for some time past, to write an orderly account to you'.

This is interesting but baffling, for there are some ambiguities and not much information. Who were those who had written previously? Was their work completed? Was it satisfactory? How much of the life of Jesus did they cover? How much of the annunciation and nativity? How many were eyewitnesses? Why did Luke, who was not an eyewitness, indeed probably a Gentile, feel the need to compile another narrative? Is he

---

[1] *The Birth of the Messiah*, p. 497

26

seeking to introduce order into chaos? Such a formal preface is unique in the Bible in following an established Greek convention, and it may indicate that Luke understood his work as literature.[2]

It is generally held that Luke, like Matthew, had before him Mark's Gospel, which had no nativity stories. Formerly the existence of Q (*quelle*, source) was also assumed, a collection of teachings of Jesus which was used by both Matthew and Luke, but which again had no nativity narratives. In recent years some scholars have suggested that Matthew's Gospel was already written and that Luke used it, instead of Q. But if this were so, then the version of Matthew would have contained no infancy tales, or Luke decided to ignore them, for the accounts of the Annunciation and Nativity in Matthew and Luke have hardly any points of contact. Luke writes blithely in ignorance or disregard of Matthew, and if he has statements which might suggest a virginal conception then they are indicated in a quite different fashion from those of Matthew. As C. F. Evans puts it, 'if the Lukan birth stories are to be adjudged a retelling of those in Matthew . . . it will have involved, not the revision of Matthew's stories but their disappearance without trace and their total replacement'.[3]

The early Christian circles from which Luke obtained his narratives, or in which he and others elaborated them, while different from those of Matthew yet had some similar preoccupations. There are fulfilments of divine words, and there appear angelic messengers to Zechariah, Mary and the shepherds. In fact, whereas the angels speak to Joseph in dreams in Matthew's accounts, according to Luke they are embodied and named: 'standing on the right side of the altar of incense' for Zechariah and named as Gabriel; coming again as Gabriel to Nazareth to Mary; and an angelic speaker with a multitude of the heavenly host appearing to the shepherds and afterwards going away from them into heaven. In the whole Bible Gabriel is only named here and in the late book of Daniel (8, 16; 9, 21).

[2]C. F. Evans, *Saint Luke*, p. 116
[3]*ibid.*, p. 24.

Even if Luke is a Gentile, the narratives he presents have much in common with Old Testament stories, no doubt as they were studied in the early church. The clearest parallel to the tales of Zechariah and Mary is the annunciation to Hannah, who was barren but received the child Samuel in answer to her prayers and then vowed him to the service of God. The Magnificat, put into the mouth of Mary (or Elizabeth in some manuscripts) in Luke 1, 46-55, is similar to the song of Hannah in 1 Samuel 2; though it is remarkable that it contains no reference to a virginal conception.

* * * * *

Luke, alone in the New Testament, provides the stories of the angelic appearance and annunciation to the priest Zechariah, the conception by his wife Elizabeth, and the birth of John the Baptist. Elizabeth is said to be one of 'the daughters of Aaron', a Levite, of the priestly tribe, and later she is said to be 'kinswoman' to Mary, who apparently would thus also be a Levite (1, 36). So it has been remarked that 'there emerges here alone, and almost casually', that there was a physical relationship between Jesus and John the Baptist 'on the mother's side'. This would rule out Mary from a Davidic genealogy, but it may also reflect something of the relationships said to have existed between the followers of Jesus and those of John. But some scholars question the historical basis for the kinship of Jesus and John, and it seems to be denied also in the fourth Gospel ('I myself did not know him', the Baptist is said to have remarked of Jesus, John 1, 31).

The annunciation to Zechariah is like that to Abraham, but it should also be compared with the annunciation to Mary. Luke says that Zechariah was 'advanced in years', 'an old man' (1, 7 and 18), implying his impotence, but the angelic promise indicated that he would be invigorated by God. His wife Elizabeth had not only been 'barren', but she was now also 'advanced in years', past the menopause, like Abraham's wife Sarah.

When the angel promised the couple the birth of a son, Zechariah was incredulous and so was stricken dumb till the birth of John, 'because you did not believe my words'. When Elizabeth conceived she rejoiced that God had taken away her 'reproach among men', and yet surprisingly she hid herself for five months. The notion of concealment perhaps matches Zechariah's dumbness, but in the sixth month Gabriel told Mary that Elizabeth was pregnant and the two women met and rejoiced together.

Elizabeth and Mary are in contrast to each other. The former at the end of life, barren and past bearing, till activated by divine power on both her and her husband. Mary is at the beginning of her adult life, a virgin, till overshadowed by a power of the Most High, and she is betrothed to Joseph of the house of David.

JUDAH TRIBE

* * * * *

In Luke's narrative of the annunciation to Mary, apparently a Levite, the angel promises that God will give her son 'the throne of his father David' (1, 32). Since David was of the tribe of Judah, this promise could only be fulfilled through the succession of that tribe, and it had just been stated that Mary was engaged to Joseph of the Davidic house. Some writers have suggested that one of Mary's parents might have come from the tribe of Judah, but there is no evidence for such a speculation. As with the genealogy, the tradition here is that succession goes through Joseph.

The angel Gabriel promises Mary that 'you will conceive in your womb and bear a son' (1, 31), and Mary responds, 'How can this be, since I do not know a man?' The Revised Standard Version and some other modern English translations render these words as 'I have no husband'. But critics point out that 'this euphemistic translation is incorrect and obscures the difficulties'.[4]

Commentators continue that 'it is remarkable that the question, though standing at the kernel of the story, should be barely intelligible, and have led to such tortuous exegesis'.[5]

---

[4]C.F. Evans, p. 162.
[5]loc. cit.

Mary's question might make sense if there had been no previous mention of a man, but in fact the engagement to Joseph had been plainly stated and they would expect to have sexual relations in due course.

Several interpretations of this verse have been suggested. One is that although Mary was betrothed, the conception would take place at once, without Joseph's participation. But the angel's words, 'you will conceive in your womb', refer to the future and do not imply immediate conception, or even necessarily conception before marriage.

Another interpretation, from patristic and later Roman Catholic writers, but now increasingly abandoned, was to suggest that Mary's question indicated the future as well as the past, making a vow of lifelong virginity, 'since I shall never know a man sexually'. This view was heavily influenced by the later but unbiblical belief in the perpetual virginity of Mary. But this is not what the text says, and it has already been shown on Matthew 1, 25 that such a theory has no support in Matthew either.[6]

It has also been suggested that Mary's question might be linked with Isaiah 7, 14, 'the young woman' or 'the virgin' (in Greek translation) 'shall conceive'. But Luke never quotes this verse, and we have noted previously that its use in Matthew is highly questionable.

To Gabriel Zechariah had said, 'How shall I know this?' and to Gabriel also Mary questions, 'How can this be?' It may well be that Mary's query is 'a literary device', thus giving Gabriel the opportunity to develop his message, as he had done with Zechariah according to this story.

Mary's betrothal to Joseph may indicate that she is a minor in the eyes of Jewish law, or according to Luke, awaiting the biological change to the condition of wife. So her question to the angel might mean, 'I am not yet ready for marriage', or 'I have not yet begun to menstruate', or simply 'I am too young'.[7] And the angel replies that a similar biological difficulty, at the other end of life, had been present for her cousin Elizabeth

---

[6] see p. 15f. above.
[7] G. Vermes, *Jesus the Jew*, p. 221.

who had conceived by her husband, although she was too old and past the menopause, 'for with God nothing is impossible'.

The angel tells Mary that 'holy spirit will come upon you, and power of the Highest'. These are general terms for supernatural strength and blessing such as have already come upon Elizabeth. There are no definite articles for 'holy spirit' here, just as in Matthew 1, 20; and it was remarked on that verse that it can be misleading to insert definite articles and capital letters in the manner of modern translators which suggest later Trinitarian theology.

The promised child 'will be called holy, son of God', again no definite article or capital letter. It should be repeated, as on Matthew, that the use of the word 'holy' does not suggest that the divine action, or blessing, would exempt the child from inherited or original sin. Such a notion does not appear.

The Roman Catholic scholar J. A. Fitzmyer has argued that Luke's story does not contain the idea of a virginal conception. 'When this account is read in and for itself — without the overtones of the Matthean annunciation to Joseph — every detail of it could be understood of a child to be born to Mary in the usual human way'.[8] On an independent and natural reading of Luke's narrative, Mary would become pregnant, with Joseph as father of her child. The conception would still be regarded as the divine blessing, since in Luke's eyes an angel had foretold the coming birth and said that the child would have a unique role as son of God.

It is by comparison and interweaving with Matthew that Luke also has been taken to suggest that Mary remained a virgin until the birth of her firstborn, and yet there are many other differences between the stories of the two evangelists. In Luke, Mary is told before her pregnancy that she will conceive and bear a son, but in Matthew she 'was found to be with child', probably after at least three months of pregnancy. Surely there were not two annunciations, one to Mary in advance and one to Joseph months later? Would not Mary's first reaction be to tell the wonderful news of the angelic visit and promise to her

[8]'The Virginal Conception of Jesus in the New Testament', *Theological Studies* 34 (1973), p. 566-7.

fiancé? And surely the couple would proceed to consummate their union as soon as possible?

Not only may Luke's account be free of the notion of virginal conception, but such an idea does not seem to have surfaced in the Christian community until the appearance of Matthew's Gospel in the last quarter of the first century. All four Gospels indicate that the family of Jesus, his brothers and sisters, and even his mother, could not credit his divine mission during his ministry. There is no hint that Mary understood who Jesus was, or that she and Joseph communicated knowledge of a special conception or birth to the early disciples. Only after the resurrection did the apostles declare that Jesus had *become* the Messiah, or the Son of God, and that without mentioning a virginal conception.[9]

* * * * *

To place the words said to have been spoken to Mary in context, with phrases used by Biblical writers, it may be interesting to compare promises made and statements used of other women in the Bible.

According to Genesis when Eve brought forth Cain she said, 'I have gotten a man with the help of the Lord' (Genesis 4, 1).

When Sarah was told that she would have a son, although it had ceased to be with her after the manner of women, she laughed and said, 'Shall I bear a child, now that I am old?' But the reply came, 'Is anything too hard for the Lord? At the set time I will return to you' (Genesis 18, 13-14).

Rebecca was barren, but Isaac prayed for his wife 'and the Lord answered his prayer, and Rebecca conceived' (Genesis 25, 21).

Rachel also was barren for a long time, while her husband Jacob took other women, but finally God remembered her and opened her womb. When she bore a son she said, 'God has taken away my reproach' (Genesis 30, 22-23).

One of the most remarkable examples was the mother, unnamed, of Samson. An angel appeared to her and said, 'You

---

[9] *The Birth of the Messiah*, p. 526.

are barren and have no child, but you will conceive and bear a son.' She told her husband and he prayed that the angel might come again, and 'the angel of God came again to the woman as she sat in the field.' She fetched her husband and he spoke to the angel, and then made a sacrifice, and the angel ascended in the flame. The woman bore a son and called him Samson, and the Lord blessed him, and the spirit of the Lord began to move him (Judges 13).

Hannah was childless for a long time, until 'the Lord remembered her'. Her husband Elkanah knew Hannah, and in due course she conceived and bore a son and called him Samuel, for she said, 'I have asked him of the Lord' (1 Samuel 1, 19f.).

Elizabeth was both barren and beyond the menopause, like Sarah, but when she conceived after the angelic visit she said, 'The Lord has done this to me, in the days when he looked on me, to take away my reproach among men' (Luke 1, 25).

Statements said to have been made to and by Mary in Luke's Gospel are comparable with these other instances, though they are longer because they come in the story of the Messiah. Mary was told that 'holy spirit will come upon you, and power of the Most High', and that 'the child to be born will be called holy, son of God'. There are no biological details of a supernatural impregnation, or a late discovery of pregnancy as in Matthew.

In all the previous instances of conceptions noted above divine help is given: conception 'with the help of the Lord', or 'thus has the Lord done to me'. The role of the husbands is rarely mentioned, but it is naturally assumed, and so it may be with Mary, in Luke's account.

* * * * *

If the annunciation and nativity sections of Luke did indeed teach a non-human parentage for Jesus, then it is astonishing that in the narratives which follow his 'parents' or his 'father' are mentioned six times. These numerous references, going beyond the infancy narratives, contradict that interpretation of the earlier chapters which would indicate a supernatural conception. On the contrary, the stories read naturally of family life.

Joseph and Mary live in Nazareth, not going there later as in Matthew's version. For a census, 'conveniently timed', as Küng says,[10] and difficult to identify from secular records, they go to Bethlehem as to Joseph's ancestral town, with no reference to it from prophecy as in Matthew. Joseph takes Mary as his 'betrothed', though some manuscripts say his 'wife', and others have the conflated reading 'betrothed wife'. The last would make sense if it meant that Mary was now living with Joseph. If they were not living together why should they travel together to Bethlehem?

Luke does not actually mention the 'stable' of tradition, but he says that there was 'no room for them in the *kataluma*'. This word is usually translated 'inn', but in the only other place where it occurs it refers to an 'upper room' or guest chamber (Luke 22, 11; Mark 14, 14). As Luke says there was a manger in the place where Jesus was born, that probably indicates a large ground floor room where animals might be kept at night though they would no doubt be put elsewhere if the room was crowded with people.

For Luke the adoration of the simple shepherds informed by angels is given instead of the learned Magi guided by a star. There is no indication of the time of year for the birth of Jesus, and various times between March and November have been suggested when shepherds would be out in the fields. The choice of 25 December for Christmas took place in the fourth century, adopting a pagan festival of the Birth of the Invincible Sun, a New Year celebration after the winter solstice.

It was noted in the previous chapter that in Luke there is no hint of a massacre of the innocents or a flight into Egypt. The baby Jesus, he says, is circumcised after eight days according to the Law, and then 'the parents' (2, 27) present him in the temple of Jerusalem. A devout layman Simeon hails Jesus as 'a light for revelation to Gentiles, and glory to thy people Israel'. At this 'his father and mother' marvel (2, 33), despite the previous angelic annunciation, and then they return directly 'to their own town, Nazareth'.

---

[10]*On Being a Christian*, p. 451.

There follows the story of the visit of the boy Jesus to the temple, after his Bar Mitzvah. It is said that 'his parents' went up every year for the feast of Passover (2, 41-51). When they returned home 'his parents' did not know that Jesus stayed behind, and on finding him Mary said, 'your father and I have sought you sorrowing'.

The genealogy of Luke 3, 23-38, as was noted earlier, implies that Joseph was the father of Jesus. Only the phrase 'the son, as was supposed, of Joseph', suggests otherwise. This may be an editorial or scribal attempt to bring the account into harmony with Matthew's story. If the Lucan annunciation to Mary does not suggest a virginal conception, then this bracketed phrase is the only contrary hint in this Gospel.

Joseph's parenthood is explicit again in Luke's version of the query of the people at Nazareth, 'Is not this Joseph's son?' (4, 22). It may be concluded that according to most, or all, of Luke's annunciation and nativity narratives, Jesus was the natural and legitimate son of Joseph and Mary. Though this evangelist believed that the birth of Jesus had been divinely promised and blessed. Therefore Matthew was solely responsible for propagating the notion of the Virginal Conception, and even his accounts have ambiguities.

4

At Nazareth

The Nativity stories of Matthew and Luke are speculative or poetical; the history of Jesus begins with his coming from 'Nazareth of Galilee', and it is here that Mark wisely begins his Gospel (1, 9). From this point all the Gospels and Acts show that the home of Jesus had been that insignificant village in Galilee called Nazareth, and from it Jesus was called the Nazarene. Frequently in the Gospels he is referred to as 'Jesus of Nazareth', and also in Acts, though in none of the epistles. According to John, only, he was crucified as 'Jesus the Nazorean' (19, 19).

Nazareth is not mentioned in the Old Testament, and the first Nazarenes of whom we have knowledge were Joseph and Mary. Luke, as has been noted, says that the angel Gabriel went to visit Mary in 'a town of Galilee named Nazareth', and later Joseph went to the census at Bethlehem 'from Galilee, from the town of Nazareth'. Matthew sent Joseph and Mary to Nazareth only after a return from Egypt, and fitted it into an unidentifiable prophecy. Whether Jesus was born in Nazareth or Bethlehem has been much discussed, but the silence of the rest of the New Testament on Bethlehem is impressive. Jesus is the Nazarene, and Galilee is his home country.

The first Jewish Christians were probably called Nazarenes, before the Hellenists or Gentile converts came to be known as Christians at Antioch. Acts 24, 5 indicates 'the sect of the Nazarenes'. The church father Tertullian in the second century noted that a name for the followers of Jesus was Nazarenes, and forms of the name are found in various semitic languages. The name Nasārā is applied to Christians in the Qur'ān and Islamic Traditions.[1]

[1] R. A. Pritz, *Nazarene Jewish Christianity*, 1988, p. 11.

It was from Nazareth that Jesus travelled to larger Galilean towns like Capernaum, and Matthew quotes a prophecy for 'the land of Zebulun and the land of Naphthali, towards the sea, across the Jordan, Galilee of the Gentiles' (4, 15). To his home village Jesus returned when he had acquired some reputation as a charismatic preacher and healer.

What happened on this visit is the only recorded incident at Nazareth in the Gospels, and it bears directly on the question of the parentage of Jesus.

Mark (6, 1f.) and Matthew (13, 54f.) note that Jesus 'came to his own country', and Luke (4, 16f.) names it as 'Nazareth, where he had been brought up'. This is in line with Luke's earlier narratives which located Joseph and Mary at Nazareth from the beginning, and the place to which they returned after various visits to Jerusalem. Mark notes that 'on the sabbath he began to teach in the synagogue' at Nazareth, and Luke says that Jesus went 'as his custom was'. He volunteered to read the prescribed passage from the prophets for that day, and then delivered a sermon on the text.

Many who heard Jesus were astonished, asking where he had obtained such wisdom (*sophia*), and how he was able to perform 'mighty works'. They referred to his parentage, but the evangelists report their queries in different ways.

The questions were: 'Is not this the carpenter, the son of Mary?' (Mark); or, 'Is not this the carpenter's son? Is not his mother called Mary?' (Matthew); or 'Is not this Joseph's son?' (Luke).

Mark's phrase 'son of Mary', which only occurs here in the New Testament, will be considered later (chapter 7). At present it may suffice to note that it was not the usual Jewish custom to describe a man as son of his mother, though whether that would apply if the father was dead has been questioned. Note also that Jesus is described in Mark as 'the carpenter', and not simply his son. This is the rendering of the major manuscripts, though there are some which assimilated the statement to Matthew's 'son of the carpenter', and the early church father Origen denied that Jesus had been described as an artisan in the Gospels.[2] To others, that Jesus was a manual worker and relatively poor would not be a disadvantage.

[2]V. Taylor, *The Gospel According to St Mark*, 1952, p. 300.

Matthew's phrase 'the carpenter's son' suggests that it came from a different tradition from that which postulated a virginal conception. It was perhaps an earlier level of reminiscence, in which Joseph was regarded as the natural father. The phrase is followed by the mother's name, those of four brothers, and reference to 'all' the sisters. It is a family picture, in which at least nine members are indicated (see next chapter).

If Luke used Mark's Gospel, why did he change his question? Perhaps because he had already written several times of Joseph as the father, and this is now reinforced by the query, 'Is not this the son of Joseph?' The text is plain, and this assertion is in line with earlier references to the 'parents' of Jesus and 'his father', in the infancy narratives.

Luke's phrase is echoed in the Fourth Gospel, where it is perhaps the Johannine parallel to the Synoptic incident at Nazareth: 'Is not this Jesus, the son of Joseph, whose father and mother we know?' (John 6, 42). This passage will be discussed again later. Both Luke's and John's verses indicate that the title 'Jesus bar Joseph' was a well known and acceptable description in early Christianity.

* * * * *

Although his parents and family had been mentioned as living at Nazareth, and some of them were perhaps in the congregation at the synagogue, Jesus was disappointed by his reception and perhaps rejection, and he said that 'a prophet is not without honour, except in his own country, and among his own kindred, and in his own house'. According to Luke he quoted the examples of Elijah and Elisha as prophets who were not respected in the similar country of northern Israel.

Jesus 'could do no mighty work' in Nazareth (Mark 6, 5) because of their unbelief, though he did lay hands on a few sick folk and healed them. In Luke it is said that the people put him out of the town and led him to the brow of a hill to throw him down, but it has been suggested that this 'story of an attempted lynching is probably an exaggeration'.[3]

[3]G. Vermes, *Jesus the Jew*, p. 34

According to Mark it was before this return visit to Nazareth that Jesus's mother and brothers came seeking him (3, 31), and some of 'his friends' had earlier said that 'he is beside himself' (3, 21). Either in despair, or as a challenge, Jesus suggested a wider relationship with all those who do the will of God, as 'my brother, and sister, and mother' (3, 35).

Capernaum now became 'his own town' (Matthew 9, 1). It was not a large place, and bigger cities such as Sepphoris and Tiberias are not mentioned. Although more in the run of things than the hill village of Nazareth, the lakeside Capernaum was a country town and here Jesus was at home among the farmers and fishermen.

When he travelled to the more sophisticated and almost alien south country of Judea and Jerusalem, he was hailed as 'Jesus, the prophet of Nazareth in Galilee'. Peter was noted for speaking in the dialect and accent of Galilee, and no doubt Jesus was too.

Although the title 'Jesus of Nazareth' is used several times in the Acts of the Apostles, it does not appear at all in the rest of the New Testament. Paul showed no interest in the human origins and life of Jesus, yet although his influence was great in the early church it is remarkable that after Paul's death there appeared four Gospels giving many details of the life and teachings of Jesus.

Acts has the one reference to 'the sect of the Nazarenes' (24, 5), and some of the Nazarenes were later said to believe that Jesus was 'the son of Joseph and Mary' (see later on Early Humanism).

Eusebius quotes Julius Africanus stating that Nazareth and neighbouring villages were centres of relatives of Jesus.[4] Down the ages, with intervals in wars, Nazareth remained a typically Christian village, at least the older parts of it. Joseph probably died here, and a tomb of a saint whose name has been forgotten has long been venerated as that of St Joseph.

[4] Eusebius, 1, 7, 14.

5

Brothers and Sisters — The Master's People

Medieval and modern pictures of the Holy Family most often present Mary with the infant Jesus, adding Joseph as an old man. Occasionally another child may be included, usually John the Baptist as cousin of Jesus. That as Jesus grew up there were more children born into the family, at least six or seven, is the Gospel picture. Yet this fact seems to have been completely ignored in tradition and art. For theology and morality the model of the larger family has important bearings on the question of the parentage of Jesus, on Christian views of sex and family life, and on the meaning of Christmas and the Nativity for modern times.

At Nazareth it was asked: 'Is not this the carpenter, the son of Mary, and brother of James (Jacob) and Joses and Juda and Simon? and are not his sisters here with us?' (Mark 6, 3). Matthew (13, 55-56) repeats this with a different order: 'Are not his brothers James and Joseph and Simon and Judas? And are not all his sisters with us?' Assuming that Mark wrote first, Matthew has made two changes, turning Joses into Joseph, and reversing the order of the last two brothers. To the mention of sisters Matthew adds 'all', which suggests more than two, perhaps as many as there were brothers.

That both Mark and Matthew preserve the names of all four brothers implies that they were known in the early church, for it is 'a good general rule' that where characters are named in the Gospel story, other than public figures like Herod or Pilate, they would be known to the circles where the Gospels circulated.

40

If they drop out of Luke and John, it is perhaps because their readers would not have known their names.[1]

There is extensive literature on the brothers and sisters of Jesus, though the facts of the relationship appear to be straightforward in the Gospels. These are important for understanding the parentage and family life of Jesus. Yet commentators have often been content to point to debates on the nature of the relatives by cautious references to other writers, without confirming or denying their conclusions.[2] So examination of the texts and their interpretation may help ordinary readers.

Three major points of view emerged in the early church, in general discussion of the relationship of these brothers and sisters of Jesus to Joseph and Mary, quite apart from their names. Tertullian in the second century, Helvidius in the fourth, and other patristic writers, put forth the natural interpretation that these were brothers and sisters of Jesus by blood, they were further children of Joseph and Mary. This is sometimes termed the Helvidian view, and it has strong support in the other Gospel statements that Mary gave birth to Jesus as 'her first-born son' (Luke 2, 7), and that Joseph 'knew her not till she had borne a son' (Matthew 1, 25). These verses would be incomprehensible if there were no further children of Joseph and Mary.

Against the Helvidian view was the Epiphanian, suggested by Epiphanius in the fourth century, by a number of other church fathers and some moderns. They considered that these brothers and sisters of Jesus were elder children of Joseph by a former wife. This theory was supported from apocryphal writings, notably the fictional Book of James (see later, chapter 11), and fragments from a supposed Gospel of Peter, from the second or third centuries. These sources had Joseph saying, 'I have sons and I am now an old man'. The Epiphanian doctrine

---

[1] R. Bauckham, *Jude and the Relatives of Jesus in the Early Church*, p. 9ff.

[2] D. E. Nineham, *Saint Mark*, 1963, p. 166, is non-committal on the brothers of Jesus, indicating by reference to Rawlinson (1949) debates on half-brothers, cousins, or the natural interpretation. A. H. M'Neile, *The Gospel According to St Matthew*, 1928, p. 184, simply refers back to Lightfoot (1865) and others for 'various views'.

assumed the perpetual virginity of Mary, and it has been accepted in the Eastern Orthodox tradition. But, as has been seen previously, this notion has no support in the Gospels, and in view of the many other fables in these apocryphal books they should not be allowed to stand against the evidence of Matthew and Luke.

Even more extreme was the Hieronymian theory, put about by Jerome in the fourth century and formerly followed by many Roman Catholic writers. This opinion held that the brothers and sisters of Jesus were 'cousins', children of another Mary, wife of Clopas, sister to the mother of Jesus. Against Helvidius, Jerome maintained that the Greek word used for 'brother' (*adelphos*) could mean not only blood relationship but also 'cousin', common nationality, or even friendship. And so Joseph too, according to Jerome, 'remained a virgin'. But there are conclusive objections to this hypothesis.

The word *adelphos* does not denote 'cousin' but 'brother', in classical Greek and in the New Testament. For 'cousin' the word *anepsios* was available (as in Colossians 4, 10). These brothers are never associated in the Gospels with Mary Clopas, but always with Mary the mother of Jesus. And Jerome's argument, like that of Epiphanius, was based upon the presupposition of the perpetual virginity. This was a doctrinal hypothesis, which neglected or contradicted the verses in Matthew and Luke of Jesus as 'firstborn', which surely would have been avoided if there had been then a notion of Mary's lifelong virginity. Further, Jerome and other writers assumed that virginity was a superior state to that of marriage, which is against the Biblical view. For these reasons the Hieronymian view is now generally rejected, except by some Roman Catholic and Anglican writers.

Many modern scholars follow the Helvidian view, that these were blood brothers and sisters of Jesus, further children of Joseph and Mary after Jesus was the firstborn. So the Anglican J. M. Creed wrote that 'Luke, like the other evangelists, regarded Mary as the mother of a family'. The Methodist Vincent Taylor claimed that the Helvidian was 'the simplest and most natural explanation of the references to the brothers of Jesus in the Gospels'. And again the Anglican C. F. Evans has written that 'in the light of [Luke] 2, 7 they would most naturally be blood brothers born to Mary after Jesus'.[3]

* * * * *

The brothers, and sometimes sisters also, of Jesus are mentioned as such elsewhere in the Gospels and Epistles. All three Synoptics say that 'his mother and brothers' came to Jesus (Matthew 12, 46 and parallels). Jesus responded that 'whosoever does the will of my heavenly Father is my brother, and sister, and mother'. These words do not exclude his family, though they may have been uttered after some opposition or incomprehension, but they make the family wider in doing God's will. John 7, 3 shows 'his brothers' telling Jesus to go to Judea, and 20, 17 sends a message to 'my brothers' at the resurrection.

From not having believed in his vocation, apparently, during the life of Jesus according to the Gospels, the relatives figure more faithfully later. In Acts 1, 14 'the women, and Mary the mother of Jesus, and his brothers', were praying with the disciples after the Ascension. Since there were no chapter divisions in the ancient texts it could be assumed that Luke, the author of Acts, believed these relatives to have been present at Pentecost which followed immediately, and they would have received the Spirit along with the twelve apostles. 'They were all together . . . and they were all filled with holy spirit' (Acts 2, 1-4). This could be regarded as an ordination, of men and women. Even if the account in Acts is idealised, it shows that the mother and brothers of Jesus were thought to have been part of the Christian community from the beginning (see chapter 13).

In 1 Corinthians 9, 5 Paul speaks of his right to be accompanied by a wife in his travels, 'like the other apostles and the brothers of the Lord'. The eldest brother, James, became head of the church in Jerusalem, and though he may have done some travelling it seems likely that the other brothers come to

---

[3] J. M. Creed, *The Gospel According to St Luke*, p. 34; V. Taylor, *The Gospel According to St Mark*, p. 249; C. F. Evans, *Saint Luke*, p. 377. See also M. D. Hooker, *The Gospel According to St Mark*, 1991, p.153.

Paul's mind 'as particularly good examples of his point because of the reputation of the *other brothers* as travelling missionaries'.[4]

James is named first among the well known brothers of Jesus of Nazareth, in the lists in both Mark and Matthew. In 1 Corinthians 15, 7 it is written that the risen Christ 'appeared to James, then to all the apostles' (after Peter). This appearance to James is not mentioned in the canonical Gospels, but in the apocryphal Gospel according to the Hebrews it was said that the 'Lord went to James and appeared to him. For James had sworn that he would not eat bread from that hour in which he had drunk of the cup of the Lord until he should see him risen from the dead among those that sleep.'[5] This seems to confuse James the brother of Jesus, with the apostle James, brother of John, but the story was recounted later by Jerome and it shows a continuation of the hint that Paul had given of an appearance to James which would have given him authority to lead the church in Jerusalem.

Paul includes James among the apostles, and this appears further when he describes a visit to Jerusalem to see Peter, but 'I saw none of the other apostles, except James the Lord's brother' (Galatians 1, 19). He says also that 'James and Cephas and John, who were reputed to be pillars' of the church gave him the right hand of fellowship and recognised his mission to the Gentiles while they ministered to Jewish Christians (Galatians 2, 9). James in particular appears as leader of those Christians who were strict in observance of the law, for when Peter went to visit Paul in Antioch later they ate with the Gentiles at first, but then 'certain men came from James', doubtless Jewish Christians who observed the dietary laws, and Peter withdrew from the commensalism for fear of them. Thereupon Paul 'opposed him to his face, because he stood condemned' (2, 11f.).

This famous controversy, revealed all too plainly in Galatians, is played down in Luke's eirenical picture in Acts 15, the so-called Council of Jerusalem. The question arose whether Gentile converts were to be circumcised like the Jews. After

---

[4]Bauckham, op. cit., p. 59.
[5]Jerome, quoted in R. A. Pritz, *Nazarene Jewish Christianity*, p. 90.

Peter, Paul and Barnabas had spoken, 'James replied' apparently recognising the prophecy that Gentiles could be called to God, and saying that they should not be troubled with circumcision, but they should keep from idols, and from unchastity, and from eating blood, that is non-kosher meat, an instruction that would soon be ignored.

According to Acts again, on his last visit to Jerusalem Paul reported to 'James and all the elders' of his great success among the Gentiles, and they told him in return of 'how many thousands there are among the Jews of those who have believed; they are all zealous for the law' (Acts 21, 18f.). The instructions to the Gentiles were repeated, and to show that he himself was a law-abiding Jew Paul was told to perform a Nazirite vow with four of the local Jewish Christians.

Although the author of Acts ostensibly set out to give an account of the activities of the apostles and the growth of the early church, he does not explain how it was that James, the brother of Jesus, achieved such a prominent position in the first generation of Christianity. Perhaps this is because Luke was particularly concerned with Paul and the establishment of the church in the Gentile world. But traditions and details emerge in later histories.

Eusebius, the church historian of the fourth century, wrote of James 'whom the early Christians surnamed the Righteous, because of his outstanding virtue'. He was 'the brother of the Lord; for he, too, was called Joseph's son, and Joseph Christ's father'.[6] Quoting from Clement of the first century, he says that 'Peter, James and John, after the Ascension of the Saviour, did not claim pre-eminence because the Saviour had specially honoured them, but chose James the Righteous as bishop of Jerusalem'. This does not really explain the location of James at Jerusalem, but it seems that he was a more devout follower of the Law than some of his fellows and that he stayed in Jerusalem leading the Jewish church, as brother of the one believed to be the Messiah, while other brothers and apostles travelled about spreading this faith to Galilee and beyond.

The Jewish historian Josephus, in a passage whose authenticity has not been questioned, refers to the death of James, 'the

[6]Eusebius 2, 1.

brother of Jesus called the Christ'. James had a reputation as 'the most righteous of men', and he was respected by 'those who were considered the most fair-minded people in the city and strict in their observance of the law'. But there came in AD 62 a new high priest, Ananus, headstrong and audacious, who assembled an illegal council and brought James and several others before it. They were accused of breaking the Law and handed over to be stoned, or thrown down from a parapet and killed. At this the fair-minded people appealed to King Agrippa, and he deprived Ananus of the high priesthood which he had held for only three months.[7]

To James was credited an epistle under his name, and Eusebius says that 'admittedly its authenticity is doubted, since few early writers refer to it'.[8] But James's authorship is affirmed again in a recent massive commentary.[9]

This epistle is held to be the earliest document of primitive Christianity, very close in mood to the Sermon on the Mount, with a 'theology of the poor' that probably made use of traditions of sayings of Jesus. Although its teaching on the law, faith and works, has been regarded as anti-Pauline, and Luther called the letter of James an 'epistle of straw', it has also been held that the two apostles had similar views but were writing for different audiences and situations. Both James and Jude call themselves 'servant of Jesus Christ', not claiming family privileges as brothers. *DISAGREEMENT WITH PAUL MORE THAN OVER CIRCUMCISION, DIET & GOOD WORKS*

* * * * *

To another brother of Jesus, Judas or Jude, an epistle is also credited, one of the shortest in the New Testament, but also the subject of a recent exhaustive commentary as shedding much light upon the thought of the early church, and the status and activities of the relatives of Jesus.[10] Eusebius mentions the

---

[7] Josephus, *Antiquities*, XX, 197f.; Eusebius 2, 23; see also H. Maccoby, *The Mythmaker*, 1986, p. 138; E. Rivkin, *What Crucified Jesus?* 1984, p. 31f.

[8] Eusebius 2, 23.

[9] J. B. Adamson, *James, the Man and his Message*, 1990.

[10] Bauckham, *Jude.*

epistle of Jude, 'also one of the seven called general', along with James, also of doubted authenticity. Yet he remarks that 'the fact remains that these two, like the others, have been regularly used in very many churches'.

It has been suggested that there was 'a Christian Caliphate', a dynastic succession of members of the family of Jesus who held authority in the early church; but while this theory could be exaggerated it may be admitted that family relationship played some part in the leadership of churches in Judea and Galilee.[11]

Eusebius, quoting Julius Africanus, writes of the Desposynoi, the Master's People, so called because of their relationship in the family of Jesus.[12] Some of them travelled 'from the Jewish villages of Nazareth and Cochaba, passing through the rest of the country, expounding the genealogy' of Jesus, in the version given in Luke.

The location of Cochaba or Kokhaba has been disputed. There was said to be a centre of this name for the later Nazarene or Ebionite forms of Christianity, but there is a modern Kokhav not far from Nazareth which seems to fit better. In any case there was a Galilean Christianity, distinct from but related to that in Judea.

The Desposynoi, the Master's People, came to provide leadership and example; brothers, cousins, and children becoming revered as 'martyrs and members of the Lord's family'. Although few details are known of Jude, Hegesippus wrote that during the persecution by the emperor Domitian (AD 95) 'there still survived of the Lord's family the grandsons of Jude, who was said to be his brother'. These descendants 'of one of the brothers of the Saviour named Jude' bravely declared their faith in Christ, for which they suffered.[13]

There was also a cousin of Jesus, 'the son of the Lord's uncle,' Simon or Symeon, son of Clopas. 'When James the Righteous had suffered martyrdom, like the Lord and for the same reason, Symeon the son of his uncle Clopas was appointed

[11]*ibid.*, p. 125f.
[12]Eusebius 1, 7, 14; Bauckham p. 60f.
[13]Eusebius 2, 31.

bishop. He being the cousin of the Lord, it was the universal demand that he should be the second' head of the church in Jerusalem after James. This son of Clopas was informed against by 'heretical sects' and brought before the provincial governor. He was tortured for days on end, but endured it although he was said to be a hundred and twenty years of age; he bore a martyr's witness and was ordered to be crucified.[14]

In Mark 6, 3 it is said that Jesus had 'sisters', and in his parallel Matthew writes of 'all his sisters'. The plural sisters implies at least two and 'all' would suggest three or more. In Mark 3, 32 some early authorities have 'your mother and your brothers and your sisters are outside, asking for you'. Jesus replies that 'whosoever does the will of God is my brother, and sister, and mother'.

The sisters are not named in the Gospels, and it is likely that they were less active or known in the early church. They may have had families and local ties, though this would not prevent them from being later among the Master's People in Galilee. Early apocrypha named two sisters as Mary and Salome, but while stories told about them cannot be trusted, these names were common at the time and may well have come from earlier tradition. However there may have been more sisters, as many in number as the brothers.

* * * * *

A tendency to regard the brothers, and even sisters, of Jesus as *older* must be resisted. This Epiphanian view gained currency through the popularity of the earlier apocryphal Book of James (see Chapter 11), and it infected the works of great artists, such as Giotto (see Chapter 12 below), which served as instruction for the illiterate masses. But, as has been seen, the clear evidence of the Gospels, on which modern critical commentators insist, is that these brothers and sisters were *younger* than Jesus and later members of the growing family at Nazareth.

[14]*ibid.*

With Jesus as firstborn child, four brothers and two or more sisters, there would be at least seven children, perhaps eight or more. With the two parents this made up a Holy Family of nine or ten members, a much richer and more diverse picture from that of the duo or trio of traditional Christian art.

6

Son of Joseph, in John

Like Mark, the earliest Gospel, the fourth and latest canonical
Gospel contains no infancy narratives. This work, traditionally
attributed to an unidentified John, has many differences from
the first three, Synoptic, Gospels. It was perhaps written some
time between AD 90 and 140, and its contents may suggest that
at least in some late Christian circles the notion of a virginal
conception was not known. Or perhaps it was regarded as
unlikely, or irrelevant.

John's Gospel contains numerous fairly short narrative
sections, often unparalleled in the Synoptics, and these may be
followed by long discourses on the nature and work of Christ.
Though put into the mouth of Jesus, these discourses may be
better understood as compositions of a believing disciple or
Christian circle. So Macquarrie comments that 'we may well
suppose that these expressions are placed on Jesus' lips by John
or the community of believers to which he belonged and that
John ascribes to Jesus and sometimes to the disciples a
consciousness, which they almost certainly did not have at the
time, of what was going on, a consciousness which could only
emerge as time passed and events could be seen in perspective.'[1]

The Johannine attitude was significant in the development
of Christology, yet it bypasses the question of virginal conception
by emphasising the heavenly origins of the Christ. Thus it can
make plain statements that Jesus was 'son of Joseph', while
referring back to his heavenly Father in a far more complex way

---

[1] J. Macquarrie, *Jesus Christ in Modern Thought*, p. 229.

than in the Synoptics. Examination of key Johannine verses demonstrates the subtlety of this Gospel's treatment.

* * * * *

In John 1, 45 Philip tells Nathanael, 'we have found him of whom Moses in the law and also the prophets wrote, Jesus of Nazareth, son of Joseph'. This is a statement of a believer, looking back to the law and the prophets, as Christians did, and seeing their words fulfilled in the Messiah who is Joseph's son, though there was no reference to Nazareth in the prophets.

In John 6, 42 'the Jews' reject the heavenly origin of Jesus because they are sure of his earthly parentage: 'Is not this Jesus, the son of Joseph, whose father and mother we know?' This passage is probably parallel to the story of the rejection at Nazareth, recounted in Mark, Matthew and Luke.

The fourth Gospel writes in general terms of 'the Jews', sixty-seven times, contrasted with only five times each in Matthew and Luke and six in Mark. The author is a very Hellenized Jew, or perhaps even a Gentile Christian. He writes at a late date, long after the fall of Jerusalem and the dispersion of the Jews, when Christianity could be contrasted with Judaism and there were many more Gentile than Jewish Christians. But John's general picture of 'the Jews' as all opposed to Jesus is unfortunate and has influenced Christian attitudes ever since. To accuse 'the Jews' of seeking to kill Jesus from an early date (see 5, 16 and 5, 18) is not only anachronistic, it is distorting and inflammatory.

On the verses which state that Jesus was 'the son of Joseph', commentators are not clear as to whether John is asserting the human parentage of Jesus, or whether he has an underlying belief in a virginal conception. Thus in his standard exegesis, C. K. Barrett agrees that 'John nowhere affirms belief in the virgin birth of Jesus', yet he considers it 'probable that he knew and accepted the doctrine and that he here ironically alludes to it'.[2]

[2]C. K. Barrett, *The Gospel According to St John*, 1956, p. 244.

But in his comments on 1, 45 and 6, 42, quoted above, Barrett only deals with the second passage: 'the disbelieving Jews speak of Jesus as the son of Joseph, a relationship which discredits his claim to have come down from heaven ... It is in accord with his ironical use of traditional material that he should allow Jesus to be ignorantly described as "son of Joseph".[3] Yet the first passage, of words attributed to Philip, is not from the 'disbelieving' nor an ignorant description, it is said to come from a disciple. Both passages deserve fuller treatment, with examination of John's theological standpoints.

Since John probably knew Mark's Gospel, which ignores the birth of Jesus, but perhaps did not know Matthew or Luke, at least in their full forms, the assumption that John believed Jesus to have had 'no human father' seems unwarranted. Further, since Mark refers to Jesus as 'son of Mary' (Mark 6, 3, the only place where this title is used in the New Testament), it is remarkable that John prefers 'son of Joseph' in the parallel passage.

Indeed the whole bearing of the passages in John seems to be that critics were missing the point, and even disciples may not have realised the whole truth. The complex Johannine theology looks beyond detail to principle. Critics and friends alike may have known the parentage of Jesus, human and located, but they were blind to his heavenly origin. When Jesus is said to have declared that 'I am the bread which came down from heaven', all people could say was, 'We know your father and mother, you are Joseph's boy'. They could not understand the real nature of the Christ, the Logos, because 'no one can come to me unless the Father who sent me draws him' (6, 44). This is the heavenly Father, though Joseph is not denied.

It may fairly be held that the notion of a virginal conception would be regarded by John as irrelevant, if he had heard of it, because it was not the real issue. The nativity stories could be considered as heavy-handed, or even magical, misinterpretations of the central concern, which was that 'the Word became flesh'. This assertion was quite independent of any gynaecological speculations. John, like the Synoptics and

---

[3]*ibid.*, p. 153.

Judaism in general, did not regard sex as unclean or inferior, for it was given by God. The Word becoming flesh must follow the natural channel provided by the Creator.

* * * * *

Not only 'the Jews' but also Christian commentators have often been wide of the mark. John 1, 12-13 states that 'to as many as received him, who believed in his name, he gave power to become children of God; who were born, not of blood, nor of the will of the flesh, nor of the will of man, but of God'. It should not be necessary to spell out here that all human beings, including Jesus, were born of the flesh; but according to John they also needed a spiritual birth.

Yet some early patristic writers changed the plural 'who were born' to the singular 'who was born', thus applying this passage to Jesus and introducing a hint of the Virginal Conception, which nevertheless is nowhere explicitly mentioned by John . But the plural reading is demanded by the sense of the whole passage, which applies to believers, and which follows from the plural of 'as many' or 'all' who 'received and believed.' So R.E. Brown notes that 'this variant is not attested in even one Greek ms. of the Gospel, and is plausibly a change made in the patristic period in order to enhance the christological utility of the text'[4]

C.K. Barrett seems to want it both ways, stating that the origin of the variant text is understandable, and the threefold negation of blood and flesh and man 'seemed to correspond exactly with the Church's belief about the birth of Jesus.' Yet, 'since the Virgin Birth is nowhere expressly mentioned in John . . . the reading which refers explicitly to the birth of Jesus is to be rejected'. Despite this Barrett claims that 'it remains probable that John was alluding to Jesus' birth'.[5]

But only in the broadest sense can this be true, for the passage does not exclude normal birth for everybody else, and John's theological approach is quite different from that of speculations about conception and birth.

[4]*The Birth of the Messiah*, p. 520
[5]Barrett, op. cit., p. 137.

For the writer of the fourth Gospel the details of the birth of Christ would have been irrelevant; all that mattered was that 'the Word became flesh'. So with the believer, he was born of the flesh but he must be born again, born of the Spirit (3, 3-8).

* * * * *

The same attitude underlies John's references to Jesus coming from Nazareth and Galilee, or needful birth at Bethlehem. Objections to his human birth, provincial location, or obscure provenance are brushed aside by affirming his divine origins.

He is undoubtedly 'Jesus of Nazareth' (1, 45), yet Nathanael is made to query 'can anything good come out of Nazareth?' as if it were either too obscure or notorious. When Jesus is arrested in the garden he admits twice that he is indeed 'Jesus of Nazareth' (18, 5-7). And at the cross John alone includes in the inscription the name 'Jesus of Nazareth' (19, 19).

There is similar admission of the obscurity of Galilee, without a justification from prophecy such as Matthew gives (Matthew 4, 15). So John allows the question, 'Is the Christ to come from Galilee?' and 'Search and you will see that no prophet is to rise from Galilee' (7, 41 and 52). But they did not know that the real nature of Christ is independent of the province.

John even seems to bypass a favourite early Christian claim for a physical descent of Jesus from David, which preoccupied the other Gospels and Paul. He allows the objection, 'has not the scripture said that the Christ is descended from David?' (7, 42), and a negative answer either for the scripture or for the ancestry of Jesus could be admitted, because irrelevant.

Descent of David was tied to birth at Bethlehem, apparently; the Christ 'comes from Bethlehem, the village where David was'. Matthew and Luke had affirmed a birth at Bethlehem, though in different ways, and John suggests a path by which Bethlehem may have found its way into the Christian tradition. But Brown affirms that 'John's knowledge of birth at Bethlehem is unsure, and that has nothing to do with a knowledge of the virginal conception'.[6]

[6]Brown, op. cit., p. 520.

John ironically reports the objection, 'we know where this man comes from; and when the Christ appears, nobody will know where he comes from' (7, 27). John is well known for his irony, and he shows the folly of debate over whether Jesus should come from Bethlehem, or whether he actually came from obscure Galilee and Nazareth. The truth was that he came from God. John sometimes leaves the objections of opponents unanswered, because the Christian reader should be able to see the fallacies of textual arguments compared with spiritual truths.

The critics did not 'know': Nazareth or Galilee, David or Bethlehem, were geographical or lineal distractions. All could conceal the central faith in the life and light made flesh. Indeed, incarnation demands limitations, locality, particularity, even ignorance, and it does not require magically inspired distortions to fit into words of prophecy literally. Matthew, especially, could have learnt from this viewpoint.

It may be that John was right, in one way. For seeking to prove the Messiahship of Jesus by denying him a human father, straining prophecy to take him to Bethlehem or Egypt, concealing the obscurity of Nazareth, may be at best misguided efforts of imagination, or at worst a lack of faith, the faith that the Word was made flesh.

However, the fourth Gospel has its own problems for the modern reader. In seeking to minimize or deny the objections to natural infancy of Jesus in Galilee, it tends towards the opposite positions of supernaturalism or abstraction. 'The prologue of John goes much further. There the *son of God* is not a miracle-working Hasid, or a son by adoption. He is *son of God* by nature, he who manifested on earth the splendour of the Godhead, the eternal Logos'.[7]

As the fourth Gospel continues, this idealisation of Christ develops. Many of the actions and discourses attributed to Jesus in John are far removed from his works and words as recorded in the Synoptic Gospels. There are attitudes and statements in the long and complex discussions of the fourth Gospel which seem distant from Jesus of Nazareth.

[7]G. Vermes, *Jesus the Jew*, p. 212.

7

Son of Mary

Jesus is called Son of Joseph in Luke and John, and Son of the carpenter in Matthew. Yet in Mark, the oldest Gospel, he is called Son of Mary, the only appearance of this title in the New Testament: 'Is not this the carpenter, the son of Mary?' (6, 3; see also chapter 4 above). Could this be seen as eliminating Joseph, a covert reference to a virginal conception?

This rendering of the verse in Mark comes from the major codices of the New Testament, but a third century papyrus (P45, and some others of later date) renders the question as 'Is not this the son of the carpenter and of Mary?' This suggests a verbal assimilation of the text to Matthew's version, 'Is not this the son of the carpenter? Is not his mother called Mary?' (Matthew 13, 55). Some scholars think that Matthew would not have used this phrase unless it had already stood in Mark.[1] Yet some early writers disliked calling Jesus himself a carpenter, and they preferred to use the phrase 'son of the carpenter', so that it seems more likely that the standard version of Mark's text was changed from supposed motives of reverence.

The use of the title Son of Mary is a puzzle, though Mary's motherhood was undoubted. It is notable that Mark and Matthew here refer to Mary, whereas Luke and John in parallel passages mention Joseph. Apart from the birth narratives of Matthew and Luke, which have their own inconsistencies, there would seem to be no obvious reason to reverse the normal Semitic usage and refer to Jesus as his mother's son, instead of his father's.

[1] V. Taylor, *The Gospel According to St Mark*, p. 300.

Some commentators have suggested that there were insulting implications in the title Son of Mary used, according to Mark, as a description of Jesus by critics at Nazareth. So it is claimed that this title, 'if the right reading, is difficult, since among Jews a man was not denoted the son of his mother unless illegitimate'.[2] But while an illegitimate son bore his mother's name, because a bastard had no recognised father, in some cultures and in later Jewish custom, there seems to be no proof that the idea obtained in the time of Jesus and there is no evidence for it in the Old Testament or in rabbinical literature. So that R. E. Brown notes that 'Mark 6, 3 offers no firm support for a Jewish charge of illegitimacy during the ministry or even at a period contemporary with the evangelists'.[3]

Some writers have taken the charge farther and invoked general oriental custom. Thus it has been said that the title Son of Mary was 'most unnatural, and was presumably meant to be derogatory in the highest degree. No man in the East, whether his father were living or not, would be known familiarly by reference to his mother . . . except presumably with purpose to insult'.[4]

Such a view is too strong. For while it is the usual practice among Semitic peoples for a man to be called after his father, yet there are instances of the mother being named. In the Islamic world, Muhammad himself was sometimes called by his mother's name, perhaps because of the connection of one of his ancestors with such a name. One of his grandsons bore his mother's name, to distinguish him from two brothers with similar first names. And two Arab poets of the time were also called after their mothers.[5]

In the Islamic world Jesus himself is regularly called by his mother's name (see below), so that no Muslim would regard the title Son of Mary as an insult. An eminent Arabist concludes that 'it is comparatively rare for a man to be known by his

[2]C. F. Evans, *Saint Luke*, p. 273.
[3]*The Birth of the Messiah*, p. 541.
[4]R. H. Lightfoot, *History and Interpretation of the Gospels*, 1935, p. 187.
[5]W. M. Watt, *Muhammad at Medina*, 1956, p. 374.

"metronymic". Perhaps Matthew realised this fact and thought the description a mistake. But other instances can be found'.[6]

* * * * *

It is surprising that Mark, who had no annunciation or nativity stories, and so recorded nothing that would give Mary prominence, was yet the only writer to use the title Son of Mary. It would be stretching credibility too far to find here some effort by Mark to fill the gap, so that 'it does seem unlikely that this Markan reference could be to the Virgin Birth'.[7]

The villagers at Nazareth were 'scandalized' at Jesus, not because of his family but on account of his mighty works, his charismatic powers. His family was well known; his mother, brothers and sisters were there in the town. How had such an ordinary local boy made good?

Rather than interpreting the title Son of Mary as providing a suggestion that Jesus had no human father, or was illegitimate, R. E. Brown prefers 'a much simpler solution'. This is that 'Joseph makes no appearance during Jesus' ministry in any Gospel, and it is highly likely that he had died before Jesus' baptism. If Mark's villagers speak of Jesus as "the son of Mary", this may represent an identification of Jesus in terms of the one living and familiar parent, precisely since Mark 6, 3 brings up the *presence* of the family in the village'.[8]

It is noteworthy that the young man at Nain (Luke 7, 12) was known as 'the only son of his mother', because 'she was a widow'. It may be presumed that Mary also was a widow by the time Jesus began his ministry.

* * * * *

In later and modern Christianity also the use of the title Son of Mary does not appear to have been common, though there was

---

[6]E. F. F. Bishop, *Jesus of Palestine*, 1955, p. 61f.; G. Parrinder, *Jesus in the Qur'ān*, 1965, p. 22ff.

[7]*Jesus of Palestine*, loc. cit.

[8]*The Birth of the Messiah*, p. 519.

no doctrinal objection to it. It has been claimed that 'remarkable
is the way in which this name came to establish itself in the
language of Christian devotion'.[9] In fact, it seems to have been
comparatively rare. In the Litany of the Most Holy Name of
Jesus there occurs the title, among many others, 'Jesus, child of
the Virgin Mary'. But other litanies are more concerned to
emphasize Mary's office as Mother of Christ or God-bearer.

In the fifth century Nestorius of Constantinople and his
followers attacked the use of the Greek title Theo-tokos, God-
bearer, for Mary. They regarded it as incompatible with the
teaching of the humanity of Christ. Christo-tokos was proposed
in its place, or even Anthropo-tokos, 'bearer of the man' Jesus.
But the growing cult of Mary (see later) ensured the dominance
of the title God-bearer, and as the Latin Dei Genetrix, Mother
of God, it prevailed in the West.

Protestant reactions against Mariolatry produced further
changes. There was a modern hymn with the refrain, 'Jesus, son
of Mary, hear'. This was altered in some Victorian hymnbooks
to 'Jesus, son of David', but the original rendering 'Son of Mary'
has now been generally restored.

Other modern hymns praise 'Mary's child', but Son of Mary
is still a rare title in Christian devotion.

* * * * *

It is surprising that, contrary to general Christian neglect of the
title Son of Mary, it is the common description for Jesus in the
Islamic world. In view of the greater knowledge of and contact
with Islam by Christianity in modern times, it is important to
consider differences in an impartial and dispassionate manner.
What is the significance of Son of Mary, and would Son of
Joseph be understood?

This metronymic for Jesus occurs twenty-three times in the
Qur'ān, sixteen times as 'Jesus, son of Mary' and seven times as
'Son of Mary' alone or with another title. As always in Quranic
and Islamic usage, Jesus is regarded with reverence and there

---

[9] V. Taylor, *The Names of Jesus*, p. 11.

is no breath of criticism of him. When the name of Jesus ('Isā) is uttered Muslims add, 'peace of God be upon him'.[10]

When the Qur'ān appeared, in the seventh century, not only the role but the very name of Joseph seems to have been forgotten or obscured in popular Christian circles, as these affected the knowledge of the family of Jesus among Muslims. The only hint of the presence of Joseph in the Qur'ān is a reference to 'when they cast their pens to decide which of them should take charge of Mary' (Qur'ān 3, 39). This was a detail from the apocryphal Book of James which stated that Joseph took his rod to the temple and was chosen to take charge of Mary ([11], and see chapter 11 below).

In the Qur'ān it is only Mary who is related to Jesus, in two versions of the annunciation and nativity (suras 3 and 19), in which Mary alone is addressed by angels. She is promised a word from God, 'whose name is the Messiah, Jesus, son of Mary, an eminent one in this world and the hereafter' (3, 4). When Mary protests that 'no man has touched me', she is told that 'God creates what he wills. When he decides upon a thing, he simply says "Be!" and it is.' Any criticism of Mary's chastity is firmly rebutted several times in the Qur'ān, which in the main follows Luke's account with additions from apocryphal writings.

It seems that the title Son of Mary, used only once in the Bible, was not taken up by the church generally. Searches in orthodox Christian literature after the New Testament have found little trace of this title, though it is possible that it was used occasionally or obscurely. Even apocryphal or heretical works seem rarely to use it.

The chief ancient Christian writings in which Son of Mary does appear seem to be, significantly, in Syriac and Arabic Gospels of the Infancy, providing evidence that Syrian Christian contacts were the closest for early Islam.

The Syriac Infancy Gospel, an apocryphal work which seems to date from the fifth or sixth centuries, uses the title Son of Mary fifteen times, chiefly in childhood tales of Jesus with Mary, but also in versions of the Biblical accounts of Cana, Nain,

---

[10] *Jesus in the Qur'ān*, p. 20f.
[11] M. R. James, *The Apocryphal New Testament*, 1926, p. 42.

Pilate, and the empty tomb. In a version of a debate between Christians and Jews, the Syriac makes the latter say, 'This man of whom you speak, who has called himself the Son of God, is the Son of Mary'. This may be an echo of the discussion in John 6, 42 where Jesus is called Son of Joseph.[12]

The Arabic Gospel of the Infancy of Jesus apparently depended upon the Syriac, and it would therefore be later in date. Knowledge of its text comes from a version edited in 1697, based on an original which has since been lost; but there are unpublished texts of this apocryphal writing at Florence and Rome. In a French translation the editor remarks that the anecdotes in the book 'must have been current fairly early among Arab Christians because they passed into the Qur'ān.' But on the contrary it may be noted that while some of these infancy tales may be paralleled in the Qur'ān, in part, yet the very ones which use the title Son of Mary have no Quranic counterpart. So it is not impossible that the Arabic Infancy Gospel may be contemporary with early Islam, or even later and itself influenced by Muslim usage, though behind it is the older Syriac.[13]

The Arabic Infancy Gospel uses the title Son of Mary five times, in stories that are non-biblical and non-quranic, and which derive from popular legend. Since this work is inaccessible, these references may be quoted. A leprous girl says, 'I have been purified by Jesus, the Son of Lady Mary'. A demon cries out, 'What do you want of me, Jesus, Son of Mary?' The child Jesus goes into a dyer's shop and throws all the clothes into one vat, so that the dyer protests, 'What have you done to me, Son of Mary?' Though not in the Qur'ān, this story of 'the unicolority' of Jesus is found in later Islamic legend and in mystical writings. Finally the child Jesus changes children into sheep and their mothers exclaim, 'O our Lord Jesus, Son of Mary? You are indeed the shepherd of Israel', and they tell their children to do whatever the 'Son of Mary' says.[14]

[12] *Jesus in the Qur'ān*, p. 28.

[13] *ibid.*, p. 27.

[14] *ibid.*; R. A. Nicholson, *The Mathnawi of Jalalu'ddin Rumi*, 1960, ii, p. 30 (500).

So we turn back to the Qur'ān which speaks of 'the Messiah, Jesus, son of Mary' seven times,[15] as well as giving numerous other brief references. Throughout it must be stressed that the Qur'ān always speaks of Jesus with reverence, and it gives a greater number of honourable titles to Jesus than to any other figure of the past: he is Messiah, prophet, spirit, word from God, messenger, servant of God, a sign to the worlds.

It followed that a similar reverential attitude to Jesus was the rule in later Islam, and the title Son of Mary remained common among Muslim writers. In a standard commentary on the Qur'ān 'the sermons of Jesus, son of Mary' are quoted. And a cousin of the Prophet Muhammad told a story of the call of the disciples when they were fishermen; they asked Jesus who he was and he replied, 'I am Jesus, Son of Mary, servant and apostle of God'. There are many such tales.[16]

While the title Son of Mary occurs only once in the Bible, it has been noted that it appears in Syriac and Arabic apocrypha and it was popularized in the Islamic world through the Qur'ān and later writings. Yet the title is acceptable to both Muslims and Christians, for it is always used in their writings as an honourable designation.

The reference to Son of Mary in Mark 6, 3 does not in any way deny the fatherhood of Joseph, as has been observed above. But Christians might reflect on the significance of the greater frequency in the Gospels of the title Son of Joseph, indicating its acceptability to early generations of Christians.

[15]Qur'ān 3, 40; 4, 156; 4, 169; 5, 19 twice; 5, 79; 9, 31.
[16]*Jesus in the Qur'ān*, p. 29.

8

Son of David

In discussing the claimed genealogy of Jesus in Matthew and Luke, in the chapter on His Father's Line, it was noted that descent from David or Abraham would necessitate passing through Joseph. In the same way other references in the Gospels and Epistles, to Jesus as son of David, would seem to imply that Joseph was his natural father. This would undermine the notion of a virginal conception, though such an effect is generally ignored in commentaries.

According to Mark 10, 46ff., followed by Luke 18, 35ff., the title Son of David was applied to Jesus only at the end of his ministry, in the last week of his life. Matthew's references are more complicated.

Mark wrote that as Jesus and his followers were leaving Jericho a blind beggar called Bartimaeus began to cry out, 'Jesus, son of David, have mercy on me'. He repeated this call when told by the crowd to be silent. Jesus said that the man's faith had made him well, and immediately he received his sight. Matthew says that there were two blind men, unnamed.

The title Son of David was not taken up or repeated here, but it perhaps prepared for the entry into Jerusalem, which followed next in Mark. The pilgrims went up for the festival of Passover, with Jesus riding on a humble donkey. Matthew, alone, says that this was done 'to fulfil what was spoken by the prophet', and he quotes Zechariah 9, 9; 'Rejoice greatly, O daughter of Zion . . . your king comes to you, humble and riding on an ass, on a colt the foal of an ass'. The parallelism of Hebrew poetry, which varied ass and colt, is taken literally by Matthew so that he has two animals and Jesus sits on both, 'they brought the ass and the

UN-
COMFORTABLE

colt, and put their garments on them, and he sat on them'
(Matthew 21, 7).

Then the crowds cried out in the words of the pilgrimage
Psalm 118, 25-26: 'Save us [Hosanna], we beseech thee, O Lord
... Blessed be he who enters in the name of the Lord'. This was
rendered by Mark as, 'Hosanna! Blessed be he who comes in
the name of the Lord! Blessed be the kingdom of our father
David that is coming.' Matthew has, 'Hosanna to the Son of
David', and Luke writes 'Blessed be the King'. If used in this
form, Mark's statement was an obscure, but perhaps dangerous,
expression since it seemed to declare hopes of a Davidic
kingdom for the first time for Jesus, and Luke's 'king' would be
even more pointed. But the evangelists would reproduce what
they thought fitting, and they brought in David who was not
mentioned in Psalm 118. Yet David's name does occur in the
titles of many psalms, and in the text as in Psalm 89, 3, 'I have
sworn to David my servant'.

* * * * *

The use of the title Son of David is much debated and if it was
current at the time of Jesus. It is used in reference to the
expected king for the first time in the Psalms of Solomon (17,
23), a Pharisee writing of the first century B.C., which said,
'Behold, O Lord, and raise up to them their king, the Son of
David'. This work lamented that while God had chosen David
to rule over Israel, later high priests had assumed the monarchy;
but the true Son of David would come to restore the righteous
reign.[1]

Some of the Essenes at Qumran also expected a Davidic
Messiah, and he was associated with the prophecies of raising
up 'the booth of David' (Amos 9, 11), and the 'shoot from the
stump of Jesse' (David's father; Isaiah 11, 1). And before the
end of the first century A.D. the Eighteen Benedictions had
become standard Jewish prayers, which have been used ever
since, with their petitions that the Lord would return to
Jerusalem and 'speedily set up therein the throne of David,'

---

[1] R. E. Brown, *The Birth of the Messiah*, p. 506; C. F. Evans, *Saint Luke*, p. 681.

and 'Speedily cause the offspring of David, thy servant, to flourish'.

Further reference in the Gospels to the Davidic sonship appears in the debate given in Mark 12, 35-37, with parallels in Matthew and Luke. These verses have been interpreted either as showing the superiority of Jesus as David's son, or on the contrary as a denial of his need to claim Davidic sonship.

Jesus asks, 'How can the scribes say that the Christ is son of David? For David himself [in the Psalms] said by the Holy Spirit, "The Lord said to my Lord" . . . David himself calls him Lord; so how is he his son?'

The meaning of this passage has often been discussed. Jesus questions the interpretation of two passages that seem to be contradictory, and a rabbinical answer might be that both are correct but refer to different points. Jesus, or the evangelist, does not reject the view of 'the scribes' that scripture taught that the Messiah was Son of David, but he asks in what sense he could also be his Lord. In fact, the question is left open, which probably shows the authenticity of the passage.[2]

Whether Jesus thought of himself as Messiah or not, and the question is still much argued, the evangelists who wrote these accounts no doubt all considered that he was both son of David and Messiah, not simply one or the other. This comes out clearly in Matthew's rendering (22, 41-45), where Jesus is said to challenge 'the Pharisees' by asking, 'What do you think of the Christ? Whose son is he?' They replied, 'David's.' He said to them, 'Then how is it that David calls him Lord?' and so on.

The debate may half-reveal and half-conceal a 'Messianic secret', but for the later church it was a declaration both of Messiahship and of Davidic origins. This assertion is echoed in Acts 2, 34, on the same verse; 'David says, the Lord said to my Lord.'

Yet the argument, as given by Mark, could have suggested bypassing current debates by showing that physical descent from David was irrelevant. If Jesus was the Messiah then he would be Son of David by right, whatever his family lineage.

---

[2]*The Birth of the Messiah*, p. 510f.

It is notable that the fourth Gospel does not employ the title Son of David, and the nearest it gets to the problem is by noting, in John 7, 42, that 'some said' that 'has not the scripture said that the Christ comes from the seed of David, and from Bethlehem the village where David was?' John, in his ironic manner, may have regarded both Davidic descent and birth at Bethlehem as unimportant or the wrong approach. No answer is provided for such questions, because the Logos is above these matters (see earlier, chapter 6).

* * * * *

It is Matthew who makes the most frequent applications of the title Son of David to Jesus, as if this was a very strong tradition parallel to, or contradictory to, the very different notion of a virginal conception which would rule out Joseph and Davidic descent. In the very first verse of his Gospel Matthew presents 'the genealogy of Jesus Christ, son of David'. This descent, as we saw earlier, is traced down from Abraham, through David and Solomon, to Joseph and Mary 'of whom Jesus was born'. Luke's parallel genealogy goes back to Adam, and it only mentions David in the middle of the list among others.

Matthew 9, 27 has two other blind men in Galilee calling out to Jesus, 'Have mercy on us, son of David'. He has the crowd in 12, 23 asking 'Can this be the Son of David?' Strangely, the Canaanite woman, in Matthew 15, 22 but not in Mark, cries out, 'Have mercy on me, O Lord, son of David'. And, as has been seen, at the entry into Jerusalem Matthew alone has the crowd crying, 'Son of David', and this is repeated by 'children crying out in the temple, Hosanna to the Son of David'.

It is clear that for Matthew the application of the title Son of David to Jesus was important evidence of his Messiahship, and it is he who traces the physical descent from David down to Jesus.

In other New Testament writings, as will be seen (chapter 9), the Davidic sonship of Jesus is taken for granted. In what seem like credal formulas it is said that he was 'of the seed of David according to the flesh' (Romans 1, 3), a significant indication of a natural birth. And believers are exhorted to 'remember

Jesus Christ, risen from the dead, of the seed of David'
(2 Timothy 2, 8).

Reference has been made to Peter's claimed speech at
Pentecost, with its reference to the debate on the meaning of
'the Lord said to my Lord'. But before this David was quoted as
saying 'I saw the Lord always before me', and the 'patriarch
David' was called a prophet who knew by revelation that God
would 'set of the fruit of his loins' on his throne (Acts 2, 30).

In a Pauline speech in Acts (13, 16-41) David is noted as
raised up by God to be king, and 'of his seed' God had raised
up for Israel a Saviour, Jesus. Modern translations tend to
render 'descendant' or 'posterity' for 'seed', but this blunt
word reveals the belief in the physical ancestry of Jesus.

In Revelation 22, 16 the glorified Jesus says 'I am the root and
offspring of David'. So the early church engendered 'a process
of historicizing Davidic sonship', convinced that Jesus was the
Messiah and attaching to that title the Davidic genealogy. By
implication Joseph's paternity would also be declared.[3]

* * * * *

Yet the assumptions of Davidic ancestry, which may seem to
have been based on theological opinions, may have included
family traditions. The family of Jesus has been claimed to have
cherished hopes of a Davidic restoration, which had been
traced back through the exile hundreds of years before.[4]

Eusebius, quoting Hegesippus, wrote that after the capture
of Jerusalem by the Romans in A.D. 70, the emperor Vespasian
ordered that all descendants of David should be 'ferreted out',
so that no member of the royal house should be left among the
Jews. 'There is an old and firm tradition' that the descendants
of Jude, the brother of Jesus, were denounced to the Romans
'on the ground that they were of David's line and related to
Christ himself.' When asked by Domitian Caesar 'whether they
were descended from David, they admitted it'.[5]

[3]Brown., p. 505.
[4]R. Bauckham, *Jude and the Relatives of Jesus in the Early Church*, p. 376.
[5]Eusebius, 3, 19.

Another one denounced was Simon, son of Clopas, cousin of Jesus (see chapter 5). 'Charged with being a descendant of David and a Christian; as a result he suffered martyrdom at the age of 120, when Trajan was emperor.'

There are many problems in the claims of Davidic ancestry for Jesus, not least the theological influences towards fulfilling both prophecy and popular expectation. There may have been many families which believed that they had links with royal or notable ancestors, as there are in Britain and other countries today people who pretend to aristocratic links, for what they are worth.

After careful discussion, R. E. Brown concludes that 'if Joseph and Jesus were Davidids, they must have belonged to a lateral branch of the family rather than to the direct royal lineage. There is not the slightest indication in the accounts of the ministry of Jesus that his family was of ancestral nobility or royalty . . . He appears in the Gospels as a man of unimpressive background from an unimportant village'.[6]

A SPIRITUAL SON OF DAVID (v OF GOD)
TO ME. DAVIDIC ANCESTRY WOULD BE
(+ VOLTAIRE)
NOTHING TO BRAG ABOUT
"SCOUNDREL, LECHER, MURDERER"
BUT GOOD WITH A SLINGSHOT.

[6]*The Birth of the Messiah*, pp. 511, 88.

9

The Epistles

Most of the epistles and other writings of the New Testament, with exceptions like Acts and Revelation, seem to have been written down before the Gospels. The authentic letters of Paul, and probably James, Jude and Hebrews, belong to the first or second eras of Christianity. Yet apart from Acts 1, 14, there is no mention of Mary or Joseph anywhere in the New Testament except in the Gospels.

It has been suggested that there are 'implicit references' to the Virginal Conception at various places, but it is generally agreed that none of these has compelling force and they will be noted below. The silence of the rest of the New Testament books suggests that the story of the Virginal Conception was not known before Matthew wrote his Gospel in the last quarter of the first century.

It might have been expected that family reminiscences would have been passed on by Mary, or by brothers and sisters of Jesus, some of whom were prominent in the church. But there is no trace of the birth stories in other books of the Bible apart from Matthew and Luke. So R. E. Brown concludes that 'what the silence of the NT does call into question is the theory that the memory of the virginal conception was handed down by the family of Jesus to the apostolic preachers and was universally accepted as fundamental Christian belief'.[1]

Whether Paul knew little or much of Jesus of Nazareth, he was not concerned with particulars of his life on earth before the Crucifixion, but rather with theories of his divine origins

[1] *The Birth of the Messiah*, p. 521.

and the significance of his death and resurrection. Indeed Paul dismissed biographical knowledge, 'Even though we once regarded Christ from a human point of view [literally, 'according to the flesh'], we regard him thus no longer' (2 Corinthians 5, 16). Fortunately for the church the Gospels were written later than Paul, to show the importance which other Christians attached to the life and teachings of Jesus.

Yet the human birth of Jesus was affirmed by Paul and, as was seen in the previous chapter, there was the same concern to assert his descent from David which appeared later in the written Gospels. Christ, said Paul, was 'born of the seed of David according to the flesh, and designated Son of God in power according to the spirit of holiness by his resurrection from the dead' (Romans 1, 3-4). Such a statement can hardly be reconciled with the notion of a virginal conception by a holy spirit, for, on the contrary, it states that the spirit demonstrated that Christ was the Son of God by his resurrection, a view that appears also in Acts and elsewhere.

Paul writes of the birth of Christ, and he emphasizes that it came by divine initiative, yet without suggesting any abnormal conception. 'When the fulness of the time had come, God sent forth his Son, born of a woman, born under the law' (Galatians 4, 4). Paul does not say 'born of a virgin', a theory of which he was probably ignorant.

Some writers have suggested nevertheless that a virginal conception might be implied here, because only the mother is mentioned.[2] But, as we have seen, Paul elsewhere writes of Jesus being 'born of the seed of David', and in the passage in Galatians he is referring to the *birth* of Jesus, not the manner of his conception. He is at pains to stress that Christ came in like manner to the rest of his people, 'born under the law', so that his birth was no different from others. One is reminded of the debates which continue in Judaism to this day as to 'Who is a Jew?' and the general conclusion that it is only one born of a Jewish mother.

There are other verses by Paul which bear on the origins and nature of Christ, for example Romans 8, 3 which says that God

---

[2]So M. Miguens, *The Virgin Birth: An Evaluation of Scriptural Evidence*, 1975.

sent 'his own Son in the likeness of sinful flesh'. And especially there is Philippians 2, 5-11, which is often regarded as an early Christ-hymn: 'Christ Jesus, who, being in the form of God, did not count equality with God a thing to be grasped, but emptied himself, taking the form of a servant, being born in the likeness of men.'

No Trinity 1054 (handwritten margin note)

On the face of it, this passage seems to teach the pre-existent glory of Christ in heaven, his vertical descent into the world and earthly humiliation, and his return to the heavens after the crucifixion by the ascension. More simply, in popular belief, 'he came down to earth from heaven, who is God and Lord of all', and then he went back to heaven, 'the place where he is gone'.

If that is a correct interpretation, it is almost a Buddhist picture. For in that mythology the Buddha-to-be was in heaven, chose the time of his descent, selected the family into which he was to be born, entered the womb of his royal mother and, in developed myth, dispensed with the services of the royal father.[3]

Christian thought has been imbued with similar notions, and in the English-speaking world they received classical form in Milton's *Paradise Lost*, where the Son of God and the Almighty Father have long conversations in heaven before the Incarnation. Even where little read, such works have done much to form popular Christian mythology.

Many scholars have taken for granted that Paul teaches the pre-existence of Christ, but this view has been challenged as reading back later Christian beliefs. These words of Philippians may be understood differently against the background of Bible stories of creation and the fall. Paul often contrasts Christ with Adam, the new and perfect image with the old and fallen. Adam was made in the image or form of God and he grasped at equality with God, seeking to be like God (Genesis 1, 27; 3, 5). But Adam fell, to the abiding loss of himself and all his descendants. Christ Jesus, on the contrary, also in the form of God, did not grasp at equality but emptied himself and humbled himself even to a shameful death. Because of this he was exalted above every other, and received the supreme name of Lord (Kyrios).

[3]See earlier 'Note on Virginal Conceptions'.

Whether this interpretation is right,[4] or whether the traditional view is correct, there is no reference to a virginal conception on either count, and no displacing of Joseph as father of Jesus. The pre-existence of Christ may or may not have been taught by Paul, but he does not attempt to conceal the fact that the human life of Jesus was real. He came not only 'in the likeness of men', but there followed the undeniable 'death on a cross'.

In the Fourth Gospel later 'the Logos was God', but also 'the Logos became flesh'. Both Paul and John ignore the story, largely or entirely Matthean, of a virginal conception by divine impregnation. On the one hand such a notion might have been taken to fit in with a doctrine of pre-existence, but on the other hand it would have undermined the belief in the physical reality of the Incarnation.

* * * * *

The anonymous author of the epistle to the Hebrews, who has been called 'a true Hellenist',[5] writes of the Son as 'heir of all things', 'through whom' God created the worlds, like the divine Wisdom of Proverbs 8. He 'reflects the glory of God', and 'bears the very stamp of his nature' (1, 1-3). The Son of God is exalted now, but he truly experienced death, and indeed was 'tempted' (2, 9 and 18). He 'offered up prayers and supplications, with loud cries and tears', and 'learnt obedience through what he suffered' (5, 7-8).

For Hebrews, Christ had a human life but then 'passed through the heavens'. Further, this writer is concerned to establish that Jesus was a true High Priest, not by any Levitical descent like the Sadducee priests, but after the model of the mythical and non-Hebrew Melchizedek of Genesis 14, 18. Of him it is affirmed that 'he is without father or mother or genealogy . . . but resembling the Son of God he remains a priest for ever' (Hebrews 7, 3).

[4] J. D. G. Dunn, *Christology in the Making*, 1980, p. 1-14; J. Macquarrie, *Jesus Christ in Modern Thought*, p. 56f.

[5] G. Vermes, *Jesus the Jew*, p. 213.

In interpreting such stories in allegorical fashion, deductions were drawn not only from what the texts said but from what they did not. Hence Melchizedek was considered to have had no human father or mother, because they were not mentioned in Genesis. The notion that Jesus might have had no human father had obviously not occurred to the writer of Hebrews. He is only interested in the fact that Jesus was not of Levitical descent but yet had 'become a priest, not according to the law of a fleshly commandment, but by the power of an indestructible life' (7, 16).

Remarkably, Hebrews asserts that 'it is evident that our Lord sprang out of Judah', or 'was descended from Judah' (7, 14). This echoes the common concern of other parts of the New Testament to claim Davidic descent for Jesus, which would come through Joseph from the tribe of Judah. It ignores Luke's suggestion that Mary was of the priestly tribe of Levi, since the succession came through his father. That clue and the story of the Virginal Conception could well have fitted other arguments of the author of Hebrews, if he had known of them. But the arguments for the high priesthood of Christ stand on their own, and they imply an understanding of him as a man with a normal birth.

* * * * *

Other epistles add little to this matter. The first letter of John varies the theme of the Johannine Gospel, and may be as late. He writes of 'the eternal life, which was with the Father, and was made manifest to us'. And, this is what 'we have looked upon and touched with our hands' (1 John 1, 1-2).

The book of Revelation, or Apocalypse, from a time of persecution, presents a vision of a transfigured divinity. In general the Bible is reserved in descriptions of the divine: 'no one has seen God at any time', Moses only saw his back, and Isaiah saw the Lord but did not attempt to describe him. The picture in Revelation 1 is the nearest the Bible comes to the terrifying imagery of the theophany of the cosmic deity in the Hindu Bhagavad Gita, 'in the splendour of a thousand suns', like an atomic explosion.[6]

---

[6]Bhagavad Gita, chapter 11; see G. Parrinder, *Avatar and Incarnation*, p. 40f.

In Revelation it is the transfigured Christ who appears, 'one like a son of man', whose 'face was like the sun shining in full strength', who held seven stars in his right hand and possessed the keys of Death and Hades (1, 13-16). It is a vision of the glorified Jesus, 'the firstborn of the dead, and the ruler of kings on earth', who has 'freed us from our sins by his blood, and made us a kingdom, and priests to his God and Father'. It is also an eschatological anticipation of one who is 'coming with the clouds, and every eye shall see him'.

The epistles of Peter, quite apart from authorship, have little relevant to our subject. Christ is the corner-stone laid in Zion; he committed no sin, he bore our sins in his own body on the tree, he went and preached to the spirits in prison, and he will judge the living and the dead. All of this, with the reference to the Transfiguration (2 Peter 1, 16-18), is consistent with the humanity of Jesus and his natural birth.

References have been made earlier (chapter 5) to the brothers of Jesus, James and Jude, and to the epistles attributed to them. James calls himself 'a servant of God and of the Lord Jesus Christ', and Jude is 'a servant of Jesus Christ and brother of James'. Neither letter has any reference to the birth of Jesus, which might have been expected if it had been thought to be supernatural.[7]

* * * * *

The epistles were written either as relatively short letters for the needs of particular churches, or as longer theological expositions, for example Romans and Hebrews. But in no instance did they attempt to outline the life or summarize the teachings of Jesus. Yet memories of his words and works were treasured by the apostles and their followers, and as the first generation died away there was a clear necessity for written records.

---

[7]See J. B. Adamson, *James, the Man and His Message;* R. Bauckham, *Jude and the Relatives of Jesus in the Early Church.*

Despite the speculations of Paul and others, there was clearly a strong desire to preserve memories of Jesus, expound his significance, and pass this on to the expanding church, in the Greek language. This desire burst out in four Gospels, written after Paul's time, at least in the form in which they have all survived.

Although the Gospels may show some Pauline and other theological influences, and they are documents of faith rather than impartial history, they also express different viewpoints and of course contain pre-Pauline material. They were compiled, not as critical or fully-fledged biographies in the modern manner. Each evangelist has his own viewpoint of faith, and there are many things which none of them tells us. Nevertheless the Gospels provide more detail of the life and teaching of Jesus than is found for any other Jewish teacher of his time.[8] This is because of their common conviction of the supreme importance of Jesus. He was a man, lived a human life, and died a real death. But he is alive for evermore and has universal significance.

The Gospels are closer in date and detail to their subject than appears in the lives of most other great religious leaders. The nearest parallel would be with Muhammad, but his standard biography was written at least a century after his death. Accounts of the Buddha come after a much greater interval and are full of legends, while tales of Krishna and Rama are frankly mythological.

In the Gospel narratives it is natural to read of the family of Jesus, his father and mother, his brothers and sisters. They provide pictures of a Jewish home and village life. They point towards the significance of the Nativity for modern times, not in theories of celestial origins but in married love and the life of a family which can help us to celebrate the true meaning of Christmas.

---

[8] G. Vermes in *The Gospel of Jesus the Jew,* 1981, p. 2f., expresses surprise at the scepticism of Christian scholars on the life and teachings of Jesus. He notes that the evangelists chose '*biography* as their medium', and that 'no Jewish convention exists that the sayings of the sages should be transmitted in this way'.

10

Early Humanism

It is not generally realized that for a long time there was a belief in the natural conception and birth of Jesus in the early church, and this is very important for modern understanding of these events. It was shown in the previous chapter that there is no trace of belief in the Virginal Conception in the early decades of teaching and preaching in the church, and it did not form part of the apostolic message among Jews or Gentiles.

Even after the publication of Matthew, and Luke, and the gradual formulation of church doctrines of miraculous conception and birth, there remained for centuries Christian groups which rejected these notions openly and held to belief in the normal parentage of Jesus.

The Christian philosopher Justin Martyr, who was born in Samaria of parents of Greek origin, and taught in Ephesus and Rome in the second century, declared that 'there are some of our race who admit that he [Jesus] is the Christ, while holding him to be man of men'.[1] Justin affirmed that these people were 'such as have confessed and known this man to be the Christ'. The Jewish critic Trypho, with whom Justin was disputing, immediately seized upon this admission and found the belief in Christ with a natural birth more reasonable than that of a supernatural conception which Justin himself and others accepted. It has been seen earlier (chapter 2) how Trypho,

---

[1]*Dialogue with Trypho*, 47. R. A. Pritz in *Nazarene Jewish Christianity*, p. 20, n. 4, notes that some translators choose to read 'your' race, instead of 'our', but even that reading 'must give the same sense'.

recorded by Justin, provided a traditional Jewish exposition of 'young woman' instead of 'virgin' in Isaiah 7, 14, an exposition with which many modern Christian scholars would agree.

Some twenty years after Justin Martyr's *Dialogue with Trypho*, a pagan philosopher Celsus published a *True Discourse* in which he criticized Biblical and Christian statements. His work is known from the reply, *Against Celsus*, from the Alexandrian Christian writer Origen, about seventy years later. Both Celsus and Origen seem to have had firsthand knowledge of Jewish-Christian communities and, like Justin, they show that there were differences among them over the origins and nature of Christ.

Origen admitted that there were some who accepted Jesus but followed the Jewish law, and 'these are the twofold sect of the Ebionites, who either acknowledge with us that Jesus was born of a virgin, or deny this and maintain that he was begotten like other human beings'. And in a further writing Origen referred to 'those who say that he [Jesus] was born of Joseph and Mary, like the Ebionites and the Valentinians'.[2]

The Jewish Christians who held to the Law would be descendants of the church headed by James, the Lord's brother, and of other Christian communities. They differed from the Pauline and Gentile Christians in their law-keeping, and some of them at least held a naturalistic view of the birth of Jesus though they believed in him as Messiah. The family of Jesus, it has been seen, appears to have been ignorant of any supernatural events connected with his birth.

Early in the third century Hippolytus wrote a *Refutation of all Heresies*, much of it based on Irenaeus of the second century. Hippolytus criticized the Gnostic Cerinthus because the latter held that 'Jesus was not born of a virgin but rather of Joseph and Mary, a son born like all other men, and more righteous and wiser'.[3]

Hippolytus also wrote of the Elkesaites, perhaps called after a historical character of that name, who seem to have believed in reincarnation and to have applied this theory to Christ. They

---

[2] *Against Celsus* II, 1; Pritz, p. 21, n. 8.
[3] *Refutation of all Heresies* VII, 33; Pritz p. 25.

taught that 'Christ was born a man in the same way common to all, and that he was not at this time born for the first time of a virgin'.[4] This was a Pythagorean concept of birth and rebirth, and it would be foreign to most Christians.

The historian Eusebius in the third-fourth centuries, in his *History of the Church*, wrote that 'the adherents of what is known as the Ebionite heresy assert that Christ was the son of Joseph and Mary, and regard him as no more than a man.' And again, 'they regarded him as plain and ordinary, a man esteemed as righteous through growth of character and nothing more, the child of a normal union between a man and Mary'.[5]

Jerome in the fourth-fifth centuries claimed to have been in contact with Jewish Christians who had the Hebrew original of the Gospel of Matthew which he copied. He wrote that they believed that in Christ 'the whole fulness of the Godhead took pleasure to dwell corporally; not as in the other holy ones moderately, but according to the Gospel read by the Nazarenes which was written in the Hebrew language: "The whole fountain of the Holy Spirit came upon him".' It is not clear whether Jerome is giving his own comment, or referring to the belief that Jesus was endowed with the power to be Messiah at his baptism.[6]

Finally Theodoret in the fifth century wrote that 'the Nazarenes are Jews. They honour Christ as a righteous man and use the Gospel according to Peter'.[7] It is not sure whether Theodoret had personal knowledge of the Nazarenes or whether he derived his material from Eusebius. Further, he did not distinguish between Nazarenes and Ebionites.

* * * * *

For several centuries then there were Christians, perhaps chiefly Jews, who believed in Jesus as a man and as the Messiah, they rejected the notion of a virginal conception and regarded Joseph as his father. However, their views are now known only

[4]Pritz, p. 37.
[5]Eusebius 6, 17; trs. G. A. Williamson, pp. 256 and 137.
[6]Pritz p. 54.
[7]*ibid.*, p. 79.

through the writings of their opponents, who dubbed them heretics, and the details of Nazarene and Ebionite teachers are not clear or abundant.

In most of the Gentile churches the doctrines of virginal conception and birth came to prevail, and they were imposed in creeds formulated by church councils which were often noted for their bitter quarrels. The losing parties were scattered abroad, especially after the fall of Jerusalem, and their teachings were crushed by the majority which claimed itself to be 'orthodox', holding correct and authoritative doctrine. Therefore the naturalistic views of the birth and parentage of Jesus which were held by these minority Christians, can only be deduced from hints in the polemic of their adversaries.

The final condemnation of the Nazarenes as 'heretics' came with the authority of Augustine of Hippo in the fifth century, who in this and many other ways dominated church teaching, for good or ill. He wrote disparagingly of 'some heretics who call themselves Nazarenes'; five times, mocking their beliefs. 'They persist to the present day who call themselves Nazarene Christians and circumcise the carnal foreskins in a Jewish way, and are born heretics in that error into which Peter drifted and from which he was called back by Paul'.[8] Augustine may have had only secondhand knowledge of the Nazarenes, and while he admits that they confess that Christ is the Son of God, he does not refer to their beliefs about his conception.

*****

'All Christians were called Nazarenes once,' wrote Epiphanius and there is support for this view in the New Testament. Jesus was called a Nazarene, from his home village, and some of his early followers were indicated as 'the sect of the Nazarenes' (Acts 24, 5). Paul was regarded as their ringleader, apparently, by the high priest's spokesman, though he was accused of profaning the temple. It was at Antioch, in a mixed racial and religious congregation, that 'the disciples were first called Christians' (Acts 11, 26).

[8]*ibid.*, p. 77.

Epiphanius added that before they were named Christians the Nazarenes were also called Jessaians, from Jesse the father of David, showing belief in the Davidic ancestry of Jesus (see chapter 8 above). Epiphanius, who himself believed in the Virginal Conception, saw the difficulty of this Jessaian claim and so he asserted that 'by lineage Mary was of the seed of David'.[9] But this contradicted Luke's statement that Mary was kinswoman to Elizabeth who was of the tribe of Levi. The descent from Jesse must come through Joseph, as the genealogies in both Matthew and Luke show, and the Jessaians would have recognized this.

In time the title Nazarene came to be reserved for Jewish Christians, groups of whom were to be found for centuries. They believed in Jesus as the promised Messiah, expected his return in glory, and kept firmly to the Mosaic law. In the Jewish war against Rome, from A.D.66-70, according to one account the Christians were warned by an oracle of the impending disaster, and they fled to the other side of the Jordan before the Romans captured and sacked Jerusalem. But other views are that they stayed in the holy city to the end, and then the Nazarenes were dispersed with other Jews to Cesarea and cities as far away as Alexandria. In rabbinical writings the name later used for them (*notzerim*) is similar to Nazarene.

* * * * *

Some Jewish Christians came to be known as Ebionites, though the relationship between the groups is not clear and both patristic and modern scholars have often included different sects under the general title of Ebionite. Recently a determined effort has been made to distinguish as Nazarenes those who held to the 'orthodox' view of the supernatural conception of Jesus, and to reserve the name Ebionite for those who denied this and were regarded as 'heretics'. But much confusion remains, because early writers named Ebionite both those who held the latter view and those who propounded different opinions.[10]

[9] *ibid.*, p. 30.
[10] To distinguish Nazarenes from Ebionites is the special concern of R. A. Pritz, pp. 9f., 27f., etc.

The name Ebionite is derived from the Hebrew *ebyonim*, meaning 'poor people', but the derogatory nickname was exaggerated by Gentile Christians from whom they differed in doctrine and practice. Eusebius, as a later triumphalist orthodox writer, asserted his own unfair opinion: 'Ebionites they were appropriately named by the first Christians, in view of the poor and mean opinion they held about Christ'.

In fact, the Ebionites were not named as such in the first generation, but at earliest in the third generation. Eusebius said again that 'the name Ebionite hints at the poverty of their intelligence, for this is the way in which a poor man is referred to by the Hebrews'. A modern translator of Eusebius remarks that these were 'wild guesses' at the meaning of the name, but they were both inaccurate and prejudiced.[11]

Eusebius said later that the Ebionites 'inveighed against the Gospel according to Matthew', but Epiphanius wrote of 'the Gospel they have, called according to Matthew, but not wholly complete, but falsified and mutilated; they call it the Hebrew Gospel.' If some of the Ebionites endeavoured to prove from the genealogy in Matthew's Gospel that Jesus was 'of the seed of Joseph and Mary', this would be a natural deduction.

The Ebionites believed that Jesus was the Messiah, and he was not 'plain and ordinary' in their belief, as Eusebius asserted. Like some later Adoptionists they seem to have held that when the Holy Spirit descended upon Jesus at his baptism he was then adopted or revealed as Son of God. Epiphanius again, on the Ebionite version of the baptism, wrote: 'He saw the Holy Spirit in the likeness of a dove that descended and entered into him; and a voice from heaven saying: "Thou art my beloved son, in thee I am well pleased", and again, "This day have I begotten thee". And straightaway there shone about the place a great light'.[12]

The Ebionites, like James and some other Jewish Christians, were strict observers of the Law. Some of them rejected the epistles of Paul, calling him a renegade. 'They observed the Sabbath and the whole Jewish system; yet on the Lord's Day

---

[11]Eusebius 3, 27.
[12]Pritz, p. 87f.

they celebrated rites similar to our own in memory of the Lord's resurrection.' Some were also vegetarians, like other ascetic groups.

Nazarenes and Ebionites were Jews, but they were Christians also in that they held to the Messiahship of Jesus and so they were distinct from orthodox Judaism. Those who believed in Jesus as son of Joseph and Mary had a certain following for centuries. But the dispersion of the Jews, and great increase in the number of Gentile converts to Christianity after the fall of Jerusalem, with missions throughout the Roman empire and beyond, set a different course for the development of doctrine and legend.

LIKE LATER ARIANS

* * * * *

Not only among Jewish Christians but much more widely there was great diversity of belief in the early centuries. It has been shown that many Christian groups demonstrated often radically differing beliefs and practices, perhaps even more so than among the separate denominations of modern times, east and west, north and south.

Numerous Gospels circulated among Christians, not only those of the New Testament, but others such as the Gospels of Thomas, Philip, Mary Magdalene, the Egyptians, and Truth. There were further so-called esoteric or secret teachings, poems and myths, which were attributed to Jesus and his disciples.

GNOSTIC

Gnostic Gospels, relating secret 'knowledge' or mystical speculations are known to have been widespread; especially this has become clear since the discovery of many manuscripts at Nag Hammadi in Upper Egypt from 1945, and they testify to astonishing diversity of belief among Christian communities.

The Gospel of Philip has radical speculations about the birth of Jesus, for it considers the Holy Spirit to be both Mother and Virgin, and the counterpart or consort of the Heavenly Father. The Matthean account of the Virgin Birth from Mary is ridiculed as too literal and making the glaring mistake of suggesting that Mary conceived apart from her husband Joseph. It says, 'They do not know what they are saying, When did a woman ever conceive of a woman?' Mary could not have conceived from the female Spirit, but on the contrary the story of the Virgin Birth refers to the mysterious union of the Father and the Holy Spirit.[13]

There were other comparable or diverse suggestions on the birth and nature of Christ. But by the third century there were strong attempts at imposing uniformity of doctrine and discipline, with the establishment of the hierarchy of church leaders, the selection of canonical writings, and the declaration that outside the church there could be no salvation. However, this did not prevent wild speculations and elaborations, along what were thought to be 'orthodox' lines in the apocryphal fantasies, which so widely and for so long influenced both popular and official understandings of the nativity and parentage of Jesus.

[13]J. M. Robinson, *The Nag Hammadi Library*, 1977; E. Pagels, *The Gnostic Gospels*, 1982 edn., p. 75.

11

Apocryphal Fantasies

After the first century there was great development of tales about the Holy Family and the 'Virgin Mary', which had little justification from the Gospels. New incidents and characters were invented in what were perhaps pious but unhistorical imaginings. They often showed a lack of faith in the historical Jesus, and they profoundly affected Christian belief and understanding for many centuries.

While for a long time there were some Christians who held naturalistic views of the parentage and conception of Jesus, as was seen in the last chapter, there were strong moves in the opposite direction. As Christianity went out into the Greek and Roman worlds, especially after the fall of Jerusalem, it did not meet with such objections to supernatural conception that could be raised in a Jewish environment. On the contrary, there was interest in and welcome for notions of divine activity and begetting.

Elaborations of the Gospel accounts of the Nativity, leading to exaltation of Mary, and consequent depreciation or distortion of the role of Joseph, began from early times. Revealing a love of legend and romance, like popular novels, these concoctions helped to change the outlook in Christian literature, theology and art.

Officially such 'apocrypha', 'hidden things', were outside the 'canon' or 'rule' of scripture. They were recognized as inferior to those books of the New Testament which came to be formally regarded in the third and fourth centuries as apostolic and authentic, and containing rules and patterns of faith. But the apocrypha of the New Testament (quite distinct from the

Apocrypha of the Old Testament) had great effect on popular belief and some of their notions have remained to this day.

Among the many collections of apocryphal legends, one of the earliest and most influential texts was the so-called Book of James, better termed Pseudo-James. This was a Greek composition, by an unknown author, from about the middle of the second century since it was mentioned by Origen in the third century. The original Greek text of this work survives, while there are Syriac and other oriental translations and Latin adaptations.

The book claims to be by James, and it is an example of the ancient love of attaching a well-known name, preferably that of an apostle, to gain authority for the book.

This work ends by saying, 'Now I, James, which wrote this history in Jerusalem, when there arose a tumult when Herod died, withdrew myself into the wilderness until the tumult ceased in Jerusalem. Glorifying the Lord God who gave me the gift, and the wisdom to write this history'.[1]

But which James does he claim to be? Opinions differ even in modern times. F. L. Cross in his *Oxford Dictionary of the Christian Church* said that 'the book professes to be by James (the Apostle)'. Yet on the previous page he had stated that James, the Lord's brother 'is represented also as the author of the apocryphal Infancy Gospel known as the Book of James'.[2] The large *Oxford English Dictionary* states that this work is 'attributed to St James the Less'. That would be the minor apostle known as James the son of Alpheus (Mark 3, 18), but this is highly improbable.

James the apostle, son of Zebedee and brother of John, was beheaded by Herod Agrippa in A.D.44 (Acts 12, 2). James the Lord's brother, head of the church in Jerusalem, was killed on the orders of the high priest Ananus in A.D.62 (see chapter 5). It is probably this James that the author of Pseudo-James is claiming to be, but the claim is impossible. The book is dependent on the Gospel of Luke for stories of the Annunciation

---

[1]For the text of the Book of James, or Protevangelium, see M. R. James, *The Apocryphal New Testament.*
[2]F. L. Cross, op. cit., pp. 711 and 710.

and the census in Judea, and on Matthew for the account of the Magi and the massacre of the innocents, though much legend is added. Matthew and Luke wrote about A.D. 80-90, and James had died in 62. Moreover there is much fanciful material which indicates a non-Jewish environment and which could not come from the law-abiding James of Jerusalem.

Since the sixteenth century Pseudo-James has been known as the 'Protevangelium', an unfortunate title since it means 'primitive' or 'original gospel', whereas in fact the book is much later than the canonical Gospels. It is derivative, it distorts statements and pictures of the Gospels, and it adds fantasies of its own. Modern editors regard this work as 'a forgery', 'not trustworthy', or 'highly embellished'. Although he imitates parts of the Old Testament, 'the author is not familiar with Jewish life and usages'.[3]

* * * * *

It is useful to summarize parts of Pseudo-James, in order to suggest how references from it affected church cult and teaching down the ages. Here appeared the first naming of the parents of Mary as Joachim and Anna, since they were neither mentioned nor named in the New Testament.

The name Joachim does not appear in the Old Testament, but in the apocryphal History of Susanna, which appears in the Septuagint following the book of Daniel, there is a man called Joakim, husband of Susanna, very rich and a man of great distinction among the Jews.

It is a pity that F. L. Cross and others baldly refer to Joachim as 'the husband of St Anne and father of the BVM', since it is admitted that he is first mentioned in the Protevangelium of James and is rarely referred to in Christian tradition till much later times.[4]

Pseudo-James begins by asserting that 'it is written in the histories of the twelve tribes of Israel that there was one Joachim, exceedingly rich'. It need hardly be repeated that

[3]M. R. James, op. cit., p. 38; and Cross, p. 711.
[4]Cross. p. 727.

there is no such reference in the Bible, though there may be a recollection of the History of Susanna, with its very different story. Pseudo-James continues that when Joachim went to offer gifts at a festival, twofold because of his wealth, he was opposed by Reuben (why Reuben?) because Joachim had 'got no seed in Israel'. Joachim was sore grieved and went into the wilderness to fast forty days and nights, until an angel of the Lord came to tell him that his wife had conceived, and then Joachim prepared to offer extra gifts to God, the priests and the people.

Meanwhile the beginning of the story of his wife Anna resembles that of Hannah in 1 Samuel. Anna's name was probably derived from Hannah, since there is no mention of an Anna or Anne as Mary's mother in the Bible, though once again Cross and others assume her to have been 'mother of the BVM'.

In Pseudo-James Anna laments her childlessness, which is said to have brought her reproaches 'by all the tribes of Israel'. Yet she puts on her bridal garments and goes into the garden to pray for a baby, as God had blessed barren Sarah. An angel appears to promise that Anna will conceive and her seed will be 'spoken of in the whole world'. Anna, like Hannah, promises that the child will be given to God for his ministry all its life, adding whether it is male or female. It might have been assumed that this was a virginal conception, since Joachim was away in the wilderness for forty days, until the angel told him that his wife had conceived. But the conception appears to be natural, and in later art it seems to be assumed that it took place after Joachim's return to the Golden Gate of the temple.

Joachim returned, offered a sacrifice, and his sins were forgiven. After nine months the child was born, and it was a girl. Anna said, 'My soul is magnified this day', and she called the baby Mary. The child grew in strength and at six months she walked (as the Buddha walked seven steps at birth). But Anna caught her up and said that the child should no more walk on the ground till she was taken to the temple of the Lord. When the child was a year old Joachim took her to the 'high priests' who blessed her. At three years of age the parents took Mary to live in the temple. The priest received her and made her sit on the third step of the altar, where Mary danced with her feet 'and all the house of Israel loved her'. In the temple Mary regularly received food from the hand of an angel.

When Mary was twelve years old the high priest, now named as Zacharias, debated with his council what to do with her if she began to menstruate and pollute the sanctuary. An angel told him to assemble all the widowers of the people, instruct each to bring a rod, and the Lord would show a sign to indicate whose wife Mary should be.

Joseph was then introduced, throwing down his tools and bringing his rod like other widowers. There is a reminscence of Aaron's rod that budded or changed into a serpent. The widowers' rods were taken into the temple and when Joseph's was returned a dove came out of it and settled on Joseph's head. The priest declared that this was a sure sign that Joseph should take 'the virgin of the Lord'. Joseph refused at first, saying 'I have sons'. He was an old man, and presumably impotent. Mary was only a girl and he would become a laughing-stock 'to the children of Israel'. But the priest told Joseph to take Mary home and he did so. Yet Joseph did not touch her, for he went away at once to do his building, since it seems he was a rich builder rather than a village carpenter.

Then followed the annunciation to Mary when she was sixteen. Now it is stated that she was 'of the tribe of David', and according to an angel she was to 'conceive of the living God'. Joseph returned from his building, apparently after four years' absence, although he had been deputed to guard Mary. He found she was pregnant, reproached himself for not keeping her safe, and accused Mary of immorality, until an angel appeared in a dream and assured Joseph that 'that which is in her is of the Holy Spirit'.

Further trouble came with the priests when 'Annas the scribe' saw that Mary was great with child, and reported to the priest that Joseph had defiled the virgin and married her by stealth without declaring it to the children of Israel. Both Joseph and Mary were made to undergo ordeals of drinking 'the water of the conviction of the Lord', but they came through it unharmed and were declared innocent.

Some of the Gospel stories of the Nativity are included, but with imaginary details added. Joseph and Mary go to Bethlehem, seemingly from somewhere else in Judea, together with Joseph's sons. Before entering the town Mary's pains begin, and Joseph puts her in a cave with his sons to guard her while he goes in search of a midwife. He finds a midwife, and a new character Salome, and a prurient detail is added that Salome 'made trial' to prove that Mary had indeed given birth but her unbroken hymen showed that she remained a virgin.

So now there is not only a virginal conception but the Virgin Birth, 'a virgin has brought forth, which her nature does not allow'. This is the first plain Christian statement of the Virgin Birth, which is not a Biblical notion since even Matthew only indicates a virginal conception, and then suggests that Joseph 'knew' his wife afterwards (see chapter 2).

Pseudo-James recounts the visit of the wise men and the massacre of the innocents, and the problem of how young John the Baptist escaped if all the boys were killed, is solved by Elizabeth finding a mountain which broke asunder to take her and the child in, and a light shone there while an angel kept guard. Herod was angry with Zacharias, because his son was hidden who was to be 'king over Israel'. Zacharias was killed as a martyr of God and his innocent blood was shed 'in the forecourt of the temple'. (This was perhaps by confusion with the martyrdom of a Zachariah slain 'between the sanctuary and the altar', referred to in Matthew 23, 35).

Symeon was then chosen by lot to be high priest in the place of Zacharias. Symeon is said to have been 'warned by the Holy Spirit that he would not see death until he should see the Christ in the flesh'. This is a reference from the devout layman named Simeon in Luke 2, 25.

Pseudo-James ends abruptly, claiming to have been written in Jerusalem by James, probably intended to indicate the Lord's brother and head of the church there. It will have been noted that the book has many distortions of the canonical Gospels, and fanciful additions of its own, with new characters and incidents, attempting to fill in gaps and answer questions. It is not history, or even salvation-history, but its influence was widespread and lasting in uncritical times. Even the learned Origen mentioned the book of James as authority for the claim that the brothers of Jesus were children of Joseph by a previous wife, though it may be seen how dubious is this and other details added to the Gospel narratives.

Pseudo-James is chiefly interested in glorifying Mary as a consecrated and perpetual virgin. This appears clearly in three ways: the view that the brothers of Jesus mentioned as such alongside Mary in the Gospel were really his step-brothers, sons of Joseph by a previous marriage; the view that Mary was descended from David, whereas in the Gospels that descent of Jesus came through Joseph, always passing along the male side; and the view that Mary's virginity was not impaired by child-bearing, that it was a Virgin Birth and Mary remained ever-virgin. Though these themes became popular in later legend and theology, it has been shown that they have no Biblical support.[5]

To Support CATH. DOGMA

Those old Church Fathers & Popes just made it up as they went along

* * * * *

Many other apocryphal books appeared in later centuries, and they had wide circulation in manuscript and by word of mouth, as pious tales, sermon anecdotes, and artistic illustrations. These fables often obscured the Gospel accounts, but it must be remembered that Biblical texts were not easily available and they were not bound together for reference, as they have been since the invention of printing and the translation of the Bible into modern languages.

Much knowledge of narratives of the Nativity came from fallible memories, and tales were passed on by word of mouth or in popular writings and pictures. Imaginations worked to fill in missing details and to answer problems, under the pressure of developing doctrine, to which the apocrypha themselves contributed.

Among many apocryphal writings a principal influence on teachers and artists in the Middle Ages was a Book of the Infancy, also called the Gospel of Pseudo-Matthew. Latin versions of this work may go back to the eighth or ninth centuries, and oral sources earlier. It is claimed to have been written by the hand of the evangelist Matthew, and also by a scribe Seleucus,

---

[5] R. Bauckham, *Jude*, p. 26.

and it was said both to be translated word for word and also to be giving the general sense.

The first part of this composition was based on Pseudo-James, with omissions and amplifications. Joachim came from the tribe of Judah, and Anna was the daughter of Isachar of the same tribe. Joachim retires to the wilderness, but after an angelic visit he returns to meet Anna at the Golden Gate of the Temple. Mary is taken to the temple at three years old, walks up fifteen steps, and is fed daily by angels. Joseph is chosen as guardian by his rod with a dove, but he insists that five virgins should accompany Mary to his home. Joseph then goes away to Capernaum and on return finds Mary pregnant, but is reassured by an angel. After the massacre of the innocents the use of Pseudo-James ends.

The second half of Pseudo-Matthew deals with the flight into Egypt, embroidering the simple mention in Matthew's Gospel with many details. The Holy Family rested in a cave, three boys with Joseph and a girl with Mary. Dragons came out of the cave and frightened them, so the baby Jesus got down from his mother's lap and stood in front of the dragons which worshipped him. Then Mary rested under a palm tree and told Joseph she would like some of its fruit, so Jesus told the tree to bend down and give her dates. Joseph was anxious for water, so Jesus told the palm to give them water from a spring beneath its roots. Other incidents tell of the 365 gods of an Egyptian temple falling down at the entry of Mary and her child. And so on.

Many of these tales circulated in east and west, and some were attached to named towns or villages which became places of pilgrimage.

A Gospel of Mary, based on Pseudo-Matthew, is a poor production but it influenced art and literature. Joachim's offering is rejected by Isachar, instead of Reuben; on return from the desert he meets Anne at the Golden Gate; when Joseph is chosen he takes Mary home accompanied by seven virgins.[7]

---

[6]M. R. James, p. 73ff.
[7]*ibid.*, p. 79ff.

Further apocryphal compilations circulated speculating on
the birth of Mary, and her death and assumption into heaven
(see chapter 13). There were other tales of the life and death
of Joseph, Acts of all the apostles, and invented epistles and
apocalypses. This uncanonical fiction had wide popularity and
extended beyond Christianity.

* * * * *

KORAN

From the seventh century some of these writings affected the
new religion of Islam. The Qur'ān bears witness to the diffusion
and mingling of both Biblical and apocryphal narratives in
eastern communities. But since the Qur'ān is taken as the very
Word of God by Muslims, it presents problems for the modern
understanding of such stories.

Two chapters of the Qur'ān, surahs 3 and 19, give accounts
of the Nativity (see above, chapter 7). The first of these chapters
is named Imran, a name that seems to have been taken from
Amram, the father of Moses and Miriam (Exodus 6, 20, etc.).
The oral tradition appears to have confused Miriam with Mary
(Maryam). So in Qur'ān 3, 31ff. the wife of Imran when she is
pregnant says, 'O my Lord, I vow to thee what is in my belly,
dedicated'. When the child is born she says, 'O my Lord, what
I have been delivered of is a female', and she continues, 'I have
named her Mary'.

When Zachariah took charge of Mary he found that she was
given supernatural food in the temple: 'Whenever Zachariah
entered the sanctuary to see her, he found beside her provisions.
He said, O Mary, how hast thou this? She replied, It is from God.
God provides for whom he wills without reckoning.'

In surah 19, entitled Maryam, for the birth of Jesus Mary
'withdrew with him to a place far away', perhaps a hint of the
journey to Bethlehem. She gave birth under a tree (like the
Buddha's mother), and nearly died of hunger and thirst, till
the child showed her a nearby stream and fruit from the palm
tree.

Three times in the Qur'ān (3, 41; 5, 109; 19, 30-34) the infant
Jesus is said to have spoken from the cradle, and this may
appear to be fresh legend. But in the Arabic Infancy Gospel

(see chapter 7 above) a scribal note said that 'Jesus spoke, being in the cradle, and said to his mother, "I am Jesus, the Son of God, the Word". In the Qur'ān the people accused Mary of immorality when she brought the child home, but she referred them to the baby. They asked, 'How shall we speak to one who is in the cradle, a child?' But the infant Jesus replied, 'Lo, I am the servant of God, he has bestowed on me the book, and has made me a prophet'. It is possible also that there is a connection here with the Gospel story of the boy Jesus speaking in the temple and witnessed by his mother, and some modern Muslim commentators suggest a link between these narratives.[8]

* * * * *

In the thirteenth century an Italian friar and archbishop, Jacob of Voragine, composed a Golden Legend or Lombardica Historia which incorporated many of the apocryphal tales mentioned earlier, with lives of saints and homilies for holy days. Pseudo-James and Pseudo-Matthew in particular were used, and through its engagingly written narrative the Golden Legend became very popular, and influential over art and literature. William Caxton printed a version of the Golden Legend in English, which was his most popular production and often reprinted. But the historicity of the Golden Legend was severely attacked by critical scholars from the sixteenth century onwards.

For the particular purposes of this book it must be noted that understandings of the status of Joseph as father of Jesus, his age, other children, relations with Mary, and their whole family life, were almost always adversely affected by these apocryphal fantasies.

The Gospel stories themselves are not without exaggerations and inconsistencies, but confusion should not be made worse by taking the apocrypha as serious history. For history, doctrine and morality, their influence was negative or derogatory, where

[8] G. Parrinder, *Jesus in the Qur'ān*, chs. 5-8; M.N. 'Ali, *The Holy Qur'ān*, 1951 edn., p. 143n.

it was not plainly bad. There is a constant anti-sex bias, no doubt due to the prejudices of celibate writers or the growing unworldliness of church teaching.

Pseudo-James and its successors were quite unJewish and unbiblical, despite their pretence. The picture of the little girl Mary living in the temple and dancing on the altar is absurd, since women were not allowed into the inner court or the sanctuary of the temple in Jerusalem. All the efforts to maintain Mary's virginity, and bolster up notions of virginal conception and perpetual virginity, are quite alien to Jewish and to general Biblical thought.[9]

[9] M. Warner, *Alone of All Her Sex*, p. 32.

12

The Family Misrepresented in Art

'Over the millenia the great majority of the world's religious
people have been illiterate', remarks John Hinnells, 'Mass
literacy is a relatively modern and still mainly a "western"
phenomenon'. And even in mainly literate societies there
remain non-literate practitioners, notably the children. The
arts were the earliest means of religious communication, since
the palaeolithic cave paintings and artefacts appeared long
before the invention of writing.[1]

It follows that concentration on religious texts brings
understanding of only a part of religious life. In the Christian
era, before the Reformation and often after it, relatively few
people had direct access to the scriptures. The clergy, mostly,
could read the texts and expound them to the masses. But a
great deal of instruction and knowledge of biblical and
apocryphal stores came through countless representations in
stained glass windows, pictures, plays, rituals, and sculptures in
what has been termed 'the Villeins' Bible'.[2]

These many kinds of imagery drew upon traditional
exposition of stories in which the Bible and apocrypha were
mingled without discrimination. Many details were added
which seemed to edify or merely to satisfy curiosity on small
points. Critical study, even of evident late fabrications, hardly
began before the last century, and artists even now have barely
come to grips with historical scrutiny.

[1] J. Hinnells, 'Religion and the Arts', in *Turning Points in Religious Studies*, 1990,
p. 287; see also G. Parrinder, 'The Language of Art', in *African Mythology*, 1967, p.
8.
[2] B. Young, *The Villeins' Bible*, 1990.

There are countless representations of the Holy Family from the centuries of paintings and sculpture, to be found in Eastern and Western churches and art galleries, but many of them are in restricted or distorted forms owing to misunderstandings. The characters have often been inadequately portrayed, and whole dimensions of family life have been missing, due to mistaken apprehensions of the parentage, conception, birth and family of Jesus. Yet opportunities for fuller and more accurate treatment could now be open to artists and writers through modern critical study of the Gospels, and abandonment of apocryphal fictions.

Innumerable pictures show the Madonna and Child: mosaics in Saint Sophia in Istanbul and other Byzantine churches, countless icons and statues, frescoes and other paintings, in East and West. While it was natural that the Mother and Baby should be portrayed, as were Buddhist mother figures, the assumption behind many of the Christian depictions was the unbiblical fantasy that Mary was always young and though a mother she remained a virgin. There is a curious tension between her maidenhood and the child she holds in her arms. Mary often looks detached, spiritual and almost unaware of maternity, though there are pictures where she is suckling her baby, and after the Renaissance she often seems more human than earlier.

That the Madonna should become a great object of devotion was natural, suggesting a female side to the deity (see next chapter on Mary). But it was at the cost of excluding Joseph from any vital role, of depreciating family and sex life, and of ignoring the other six or seven children of which the Gospels had written.

It has been seen in the last chapter that the second century apocryphal Pseudo-James was responsible for first suggesting the names of the parents of Mary as Joachim and Anna, for giving Joseph sons already, for making him an old man who would be immune to the attractions of the flesh of his virgin wife, and for sending him away from home during the conception of Jesus. All these additions to the Gospel narratives gave an ascetic twist to the understanding of the Nativity which had no justification in the Bible. Not only in the texts but in artistic representations they came to distort Christian understanding of the Nativity and the Holy Family.

The effect on and through art is well illustrated in the famous series of frescoes by Giotto in the early fourteenth century which has been preserved at Padua. It is based with variations on Pseudo-James, the Gospel of Mary, and the Golden Legend.

The series begins with Joachim having his sacrifice refused at the Temple because he is childless, and he retires in shame to the desert. Meanwhile an angel appears to his wife Anne to announce the coming birth to her of the Virgin from whom the Messiah will be born. Then Joachim is visited by an angel telling him to offer sacrifice, and in its smoke a child appears, a detail perhaps borrowed from the story of Samson.

In a further angelic visit Joachim is told to return to Anne and he meets her at the Golden Gate. Anne next gives birth to Mary and presents her at the Temple, and then the priests are told to find a husband from the house of David, who will be indicated by the budding of his rod. Many candidates bring rods and these are watched until Joseph's produces buds, whereupon he is betrothed to Mary and he takes her home accompanied by seven virgins.

The rest of the series is roughly based on the Gospels, passing from the Nativity to Pentecost. Yet even semi-biblical scenes are affected by apocryphal assumptions. At the birth of Jesus it is Anne who leans over the baby, alongside Mary, while grey-headed Joseph sits outside. Again as an old man he stands behind at the adoration of the Magi. And in the flight into Egypt, old Joseph goes ahead and his three elder sons follow behind.

* * * * *

The secondary role of Joseph is evident in many pictures over the ages. In Nativity scenes he is sometimes almost indistinguishable from the shepherds or the Magi. Yet in medieval and modern Infancy plays it may be that Joseph is given more action, partly because of demands for filling out the story, with the journey from Nazareth to Bethlehem, and the flight into Egypt, combining Luke's and Matthew's narratives even if awkwardly. The four dreams that Matthew gives to Joseph provide further material for popular presentation.

Joseph appears more active in pictures from the Renaissance onwards, as in Michelangelo's fine Holy Family of 1504, now in the Uffizi gallery in Florence. Here the group is shown naturally, haloes are discarded, Mary and the child have grown older, and Joseph is important in supporting them. But he is still shown as an old man, with bald head and white beard. It is more likely at this period of his life, with his first child, that Joseph would have been young with black or brown hair.

A later picture does show Joseph as a young man. In the Vatican Gallery there is a painting of the Holy Family by the eighteenth century Francesco Mancini which depicts Joseph with dark hair and beard. At a more banal level modern Christmas cards sometimes show Joseph as a fairly young man, though the bent and grey-bearded figure is also common.

St Anne, that purely apocryphal figure, elbows out Joseph at times, as we have seen with Giotto. In the Louvre there is a fine humanistic picture of the young family by Leonardo da Vinci. But there is no Joseph, and it is Anne who serves as background to the Madonna. And although the child Jesus here is growing and playing with a lamb, there are no other children in sight.

* * * * *

If the older children of Pseudo-James and others are dismissed, and the younger ones of the Gospels taken into account, it is almost impossible to find a correct picture. But it should not be expected that in pictures of the birth and infancy of Jesus these later offspring could be represented. He was the firstborn of the family, and however many further children there may have been they came later, according to plain reading of the Gospels.

But in art another young child or two sometimes helped to make a fuller picture, as when Raphael depicted the Madonna and the infant Jesus, with two other children. The first additional child, here and elsewhere, was usually young John the Baptist since according to Luke's Gospel he was the cousin of Jesus and six months older. The boy Baptist may be shown with or without a halo, and carrying a cross as sign of his later martyrdom.

Another child is also present in this picture of Raphael's but his identity is not clear, though since he is older than baby Jesus he may be intended as one of Joseph's supposed earlier children.

Few artists have attempted to depict the family at Nazareth in the adolescence of Jesus, and when this does occur there are artificialities and lost opportunities. In 1850 the Pre-Raphaelite J. E. Millais painted a scene with the boy Jesus in an imaginary incident in the life of a carpenter's family. The picture became known as 'The Carpenter's Shop', or 'Christ in the House of His Parents', but in the catalogue of the Royal Academy where it was shown, in place of a title the picture was labelled with a verse from Zechariah 13, 6: 'And one shall say unto him, What are these wounds in thine hands? Then he shall answer, Those with which I was wounded in the house of my friends'. The boy Jesus has cut his hand on a nail, and Mary kneels by him and kisses him. It is a foreshadowing of the Cross.

This picture aroused great hostility from the anti-Pre-Raphaelites, because the figures in it looked ordinary, even English, people. *The Times* called the picture 'revolting' and its detail 'loathsome'. Violent attacks came from other quarters, notably *Blackwood's Magazine*, and Charles Dickens went for it in *Household Words*, though he later changed his opinion. But from our point of view, this painting seems over-romanticized and it missed a great opportunity.

In Millais' picture, after Jesus and Mary there is Joseph at the carpenter's bench, and he has a bald head. Another worker in the shop seems to be John the Baptist, but why is he doing carpentry at Nazareth, since he was born in Judea and was to retire to the desert? And where are the later children of Joseph and Mary who would be growing up now? Even in Millais' Protestant environment, with much better knowledge of the Gospels possible than in the Middle Ages, there is still a great gap. Where are young James and Joseph, or Judah and Simon? And why not show one or two girls of the family, as no artists ever seem to have done? The baleful influence of Pseudo-James is still around, with Anne and old Joseph, and there is no large and happy or quarrelling family of boys and girls.

In this century Stanley Spencer produced a series of paintings of subjects treated by Giotto, including 'Joachim among the

Shepherds' (1912). Spencer's Anglican and Wesleyan backgrounds had apparently not conveyed the fact that Giotto's sources were dubious, and he had not been to Padua but saw the pictures through the eyes of Ruskin. Spencer was not concerned with history but with interpretation, and he felt himself close to Giotto though his scenery was not Padua but Cookham. But he could have given fine depictions of the large family of Nazareth frolicking in Berkshire fields.[3]

* * * * *

Nativity pictures have become stereotyped or fossilized, and thereby popular understanding of the Holy Family has been impoverished. But if modern artists wish to vary the themes for paintings, or for Christmas cards, or if dramatists and other writers want better materials than the tired fictions of Pseudo-James, then let them look again and critically at the Gospels.

There are slight signs of change. This year I have received a Christmas card, printed by Christian Aid and CAFOD, showing a man putting up a sign on an eastern house, 'Joseph and Son, Carpenters'. And David Bromley has published for me a picture of Joseph and Mary at table in Nazareth, with four young boys. Three of them are quarrelling and pushing away their food, while the fourth, with a halo, eats his grapes thoughtfully.[4]

Perhaps African, or Indian, or Latin American artists will take up the challenge to depict the life of the Holy Family in modern ways but faithful to the Gospels. Scenes of the Nativity of course must still show only the baby Jesus, as firstborn, but both parents should be present, with Joseph as young and prominent as he would have been in Jewish society. Later the growing family could be depicted with more richness and diversity than in the past. Joseph would rightly be ageing now, and Mary with virginity far behind would have developed a fully maternal figure. The sword that was to pierce her soul would come from other members of the family as well as from Jesus.

[3]D. Robinson, *Stanley Spencer*, 1979, p. 12f.

[4]To illustrate 'Myths of the virgin birth that obscure Jesus's family life', *The Sunday Correspondent*, p. 18, 24.12.1989.

13

Mary

In the Bible she is called Mary, or simply 'the mother of Jesus', but in the later church she received the titles of Blessed Virgin Mary and Mother of God. The Gospels say nothing of her parentage or background, but from the apocryphal Pseudo-James onwards there accumulated stories and details totally unconnected with anything in the New Testament.

After the Nativity stories the only incident in which 'his mother' appears, in all three Synoptic Gospels, is when she came with 'his brothers' to call Jesus, her apparent incomprehension of his mission, and the reference to the larger relationship with all who do the will of God (Mark 3, 21 and 3, 31 and parallels). Hans Küng remarks that 'it is odd that just this single scene could have been so thrust into the background and played down in the Christian proclamation'.[1]

There is a general reference to the mother of Jesus from an unknown woman who cried 'Blessed is the womb that bore you, and the breasts that you sucked' (Luke 11, 27). But again Jesus, in a hint for Mariologists, turns the words from personal praise to a test of faith, 'Blessed rather are those who hear the word of God and keep it'.

Incomprehension by Mary is suggested again in the Fourth Gospel, though it does not name her, saying merely 'the mother of Jesus'. At the wedding in Cana, the mother knows Jesus's powers and tells him that the wine has run out, expecting a miracle. But she is rebuked for anticipating the end, 'Woman, what have you to do with me? My hour has not yet come' (John 2, 4).

---

[1] *On Being a Christian*, p. 458.

A similar address is given in the Gospel at the Cross, only more tenderly, when Jesus sees 'his mother, and the disciple whom he loved' (19, 26). He says to her, 'Woman, behold your son'. but where were her true sons, James and the rest, to care for their mother? Some have suggested that their absence indicates that they were not Mary's own sons, but stepsons, as apocryphal books later declared. But this is unwarranted and beside the point. Mary loses her son Jesus on the Cross, and finds another son in the community of the disciples. It is an idealized picture, and Barrett comments on 'the improbability that friends of Jesus would be allowed near the cross', so that 'it seems that the historical foundation of the incident is slight'. And it is noted that in Acts 1, 14 'the mother of Jesus appears in company with his brothers'.[2]

In this incident in Acts Mary is named for the last time in the New Testament, and perhaps the family is seen at Jerusalem providing a nucleus for the Jewish church, of which James became the leader. There is a famous painting of Pentecost by El Greco in which Mary is the central figure, with a tongue of fire on her head, while Peter and John reel backwards. In this picture there is another female beside Mary, perhaps intended to be Mary Magdalene, the primary witness of the resurrection. No doubt El Greco was influenced by the dominant role of Mary in Catholic devotion, but there is some biblical ground for his presentation.

However that may be, Mary then disappears from the Bible texts, or perhaps we should say that Acts and the Epistles are concerned with the growth of the Church, mainly Gentile, and the Jewish church fades out of their interests.

A fantastic vision of a celestial but unnamed woman and child in Revelation 12 probably symbolizes the church and the Messiah during persecution. But it provided imagery for the later glorification of Mary as 'clothed with the sun, with the moon under her feet, and on her head a crown of twelve stars'.

* * * * *

[2]*The Gospel according to St John*, p. 459; R. Bauckham, *Jude*, p. 52.

The mythology of Mary developed from Pseudo-James and many later apocryphal compositions, which were not recognized as canonical by the church but which had widespread effect. Much of the material on the Virgin Mary and the Holy Family was sheer pious imagination of later centuries, devoid of basis in the Bible, and with no claim to be considered as history.

Parents were provided for Mary, Joachim and Anna probably borrowed from the Story of Susanna and the book of Samuel (see chapter 11). Young Mary was said to have grown up in the temple at Jerusalem, where she was magically fed, and at twelve she was handed over by the priests to an old man, Joseph, who already had sons. A Virgin Birth was supposed, in addition to the conception, and other additions to the story of the flight into Egypt and return to Nazareth. If this fiction provided new detail, and attempted to answer some problems, it distanced Mary and Jesus from the Gospel pictures of their life.

In later Christianity the cult of Mary developed after that of the early martyrs, since she had not given her life for the faith. According to legend Mary was taken into his home by the apostle John (assumed to be the beloved disciple), who finally settled in Ephesus. Their reputed house there is still shown to modern visitors, but another tradition claimed Jerusalem as the place of Mary's death.

The growth in the veneration of Mary from the fifth century is partly attributed to the influx of the proletariat into the church after the cessation of persecutions, and the recognition of Christianity as the state religion. Popular worship of the goddesses Diana, Artemis and Cybele could easily be transferred to Mary, and psychologists have linked it with the strong desires for the worship of a mother figure. At the same time there was a tendency to push Joseph into the background or aid his virtual disappearance.

Churches were first named after Mary in the fourth century, and feasts and images of Mary were introduced in the fifth century. Now Mary was given the title 'Mother of God', a bland title which might seem to apply to the whole Godhead, and Son of God would have been more accurate. But it was taken up with enthusiasm in Ephesus, the city of the Great Mother, and in other towns. The first Latin hymn to Mary appeared in the fifth century, and in the sixth century her name was introduced into the Canon of the Mass.

Over the centuries there appeared countless lives of the Virgin, of which texts and fragments survive. Miracles abound in these fables, and special attention was given to parallels with the story of Christ: the Ascension of Jesus being complemented by the Assumption of Mary, and his Virginal Conception cognate with an Immaculate Conception for his mother.

Texts of the Passing Away of Mary, or the Obsequies of Mary, began to appear from the late fourth century, with varying details, though the early church fathers had said nothing about it. Some writers alleged that Mary's soul and body were taken up to heaven from Jerusalem and others that her soul was taken first, depicted in art as a baby wrapped in clothes. Then after her body was buried it was put in a chariot of light by the apostles, and they all went up to paradise.[3]

The Assumption of Our Lady became one of the great feasts of the church, though it remained formally undefined. Not until 1950 did Pope Pius XII, against Orthodox, Protestant, and 'even Catholic misgivings', define the formal dogma, that 'the immaculate God-bearer, Mary ever-virgin, having completed her earthly life, was in body and soul assumed into heavenly glory'.[4] But the Second Vatican Council in 1965 sought to clarify the position of Mary, stressing her complete dependence on her Son, regarding her as a model for the church, and relating her offices and privileges always to Christ.

The notion of an Immaculate Conception for Mary was long disputed. Thomas Aquinas, among many others, rejected it on the grounds that as Mary was conceived in the natural way she was not exempt from the universal inheritance of original sin. Despite this great authority, in 1854 Pope Pius IX declared that 'from the first moment of her conception, the Blessed Virgin Mary . . . was kept free from all stain of original guilt'.

It has been noted earlier (chapter 2) that in the Gospel account of the Virginal Conception of Jesus (clear in Matthew

[3]M. R. James, *The Apocryphal New Testament*, pp. 194-227.
[4]*On Being a Christian*, p. 461; F. L. Cross, *The Oxford Dictionary of the Christian Church*, p. 96.

1, 18; dubious in Luke 1, 34) there is never any suggestion that this was needed to avoid any taint of Sin. This would be an anti-sex notion, unhebraic and foreign to the Gospels. Dogmas of the Virginal Conception of Jesus, taking him away from his father, and the Immaculate Conception of Mary, removing full humanity from his mother, do but distance Jesus ever farther from normal human life. They make it difficult to understand how biblical writers could have described Jesus as 'tempted in all points as we are'.

* * * * *

At the popular level devotions to Mary developed unevenly. The salutation Ave Maria was used from the twelfth century, the prayer for her aid at the hour of death was added later, and the full invocation became widespread and comparable to the Lord's Prayer in frequency. The use of the Angelus and the Rosary grew up in the late Middle Ages, the prayer beads coming to Europe through Islam, from their place of origin in Hindu and Buddhist India.

In the last two centuries there have been new May and October devotions, Marian years, and apparitions and pilgrimages to Lourdes, Knock, Fatima, and Medugordje. Prayers to a Sacred Heart of Mary corresponded to medieval devotions to the Sacred Heart of Jesus, often depicted in gruesome detail. In 1942, Pius XII, under the influence of Fatima, consecrated all humanity to the immaculate heart of Mary.

Psychologists have commented on these developments, and C. G. Jung remarked that 'anyone who has followed with attention the visions of Mary which have been increasing in number over the last few decades, and has taken their psychological significance into account, might have known what was brewing. The fact, especially, that it was largely children who had the visions might have given pause for thought, for in such cases the collective unconscious is always at work'.[5] Even in largely Muslim Egypt there were claims of

[5] *Psychology and Religion, East and West,* 1969 edn., p. 461.

apparitions of Mary in 1967, to bring comfort after defeat in war not only to Coptic Christians but to Arab people in general. It may be noted that in the Qur'ān Mary was regarded as sinless, and chosen 'above the women of the worlds' (3.37ff.).

Jung has emphasized the importance of female symbols of divinity, the archetypes of the female *anima* to correspond to the male *animus*. Most religions seem to need a goddess, or female side of the deity, and the cult of the Virgin-Mother has preoccupied much of the Orthodox and Catholic Christianity. If Mary could have been called God the Mother that would have completed the divine family, with God the Father and God the Son. But tradition and scripture were too strong and, officially at least, theologians distinguished the *hyperdulia*, which Mary received, from the *dulia*, the honour paid to saints and angels. But both of these were less and distinct from the *latria*, worship, which should be accorded to God alone, though in practice it might be difficult to observe the difference.[6]

In one way it was a strange reversal of sexist prejudice against women, that elevated Mary above all human beings in the eyes of the faithful. And it might be thought to compensate for the views that theologians often held of the otherwise inferior status of women.

Women have found in Mary a refuge, a mother or sister who suffered as they do. In many instances Mary seemed to replace Christ, who hung dead on his crucifix. Or Mary was thought to be more merciful than her Son, who was a stern judge, as Christ also was thought to plead with his harsh Father. So above the door of a church in Cuzco, ancient capital of the Incas in Peru, the words that the Gospel put in the mouth of Jesus are taken over by Mary: 'Come unto Mary, all ye that labour and are heavy laden, and she will give you rest'.[7] It is typical of the enormous role which Mary plays in Latin America, illustrated again by the Black Virgin of Guadalupe, Mexico, whose picture is reproduced in many other countries.[8]

Yet on the doctrinal side Mariology was evolved not by women but by men, and mainly by celibates who were supposedly

[6]G. Parrinder, *Sex in the World's Religions*, 1980, p. 229.

[7]A. Wessels, *Images of Jesus*, 1990, p. 66.

[8]G. Parrinder, *Encountering World Religions*, 1987, p. 153f.

ignorant of the joys and ties of marriage and the family.
Perhaps the knowledge of the logical and biological
impossibilities of virgin-motherhood helped those who found
it difficult to imagine Mary and Joseph having sexual intercourse,
well on into their life together. Similarly children still seem
often unwilling to think of their parents enjoying sex into old
age. But these ascetic prejudices came at real cost.

By constantly harping on Mary's virginity, her motherhood,
especially of a large family, was virtually destroyed. Augustine
of Hippo in the fifth century, after his own illicit unions, was
largely responsible for the pleasure-hating sexual ethic that
infected Christendom. He asserted that Mary conceived without
carnal desire, and gave birth without pain. Pope John Paul II
has constantly stressed that Mary remained 'inviolate', a
euphemism for the notion, from Pseudo-James, that her hymen
was not ruptured even during childbirth, which seems
impossible and undesirable.

In the main, what poor guidance believers have suffered
from their celibate teachers! Much of Mariology became a sort
of anti-Mariology; for while it has been claimed to emphasize
the greatness and dignity of woman, it did so at the expense of
denying to Mary what married women enjoy, and it branded as
evil those sexual feelings which the Bible showed to be the gift
of God.

So at the end of her long and complex study of Mary, Marina
Warner considers that the western (and eastern) church is
incapable of over-coming centuries of anti-feminine prejudice.
'Its incapacity to do this is complete: the teleological view that
the natural law ordains that women must bear and suffer,
underpins the Church's continuing indefensible ban on
contraception; a dualistic distaste for the material world
reinforces the ideal of virginity; and an undiminished certainty
that women are subordinate to men continues to make the
priesthood of women unacceptable.' Therefore it is likely that
'like Ishtar, the Virgin will recede into legend'.[9]

Despite the great depictions of Mary in art many of them,
perhaps most, gave the wrong emphasis through the teachings

---

[9] *Alone of All Her Sex*, p. 462.

of theologians. How perverted is a common picture of two women! On the one side is Mary, virgin, drawn and ascetic; on the other a sensual Magdalene, with loose hair, bare shoulders and torn clothing. It is a libel on Mary Magdalene also, for there is no biblical evidence for the popular error of supposing her to have been a prostitute. She appears only once in the Gospels before the end, in Luke 8, 2, where it is said that out of her went seven demons, no doubt healed by exorcism. Then this Mary became the chief witness of the resurrection, according to the Synoptics and John. But the western church, since the sixth century, combined Mary of Bethany, Mary Magdalene, and the unnamed sinner of Luke 7, to the great confusion of ordinary people.

Hans Küng's conclusions on Mariology seem fair, that 'on the *Catholic* side' there must be no fear of 'an honest, critical examination of the two recent Marian and two papal dogmas, which in various respects form a unity and which are not substantiated in a universally convincing way, either in Scripture or in tradition or by "intrinsic reasons".'[10]

On the *Protestant* side he says that negative polemic is not enough, and that the biblical material on the role of women must be fully utilized.

With critical but sympathetic study of the Bible, a more natural picture of Mary than the traditional ones may be sketched, with real humanity. The Gospel shows that Mary brought forth her 'firstborn' Jesus, and then a large family of four other boys and several girls, with her husband Joseph.

In the Bible Mary is not the Ever-virgin, a perpetually untouched figure like the Greek Pallas Athene, but rather she is like the Earth-mother, De-meter (Ceres), smiling and weeping with her varied family. The Blessed Mother Mary is a more natural and understandable model than the Blessed Virgin Mary.

Mary should be depicted with a full figure, and with a face lined from the joys and cares of a rich family life. Whether or not she understood Jesus at first, it is said that Mary 'kept all these things in her heart'. She seems to have followed Jesus

---

[10] *On Being a Christian*, p. 462.

even when doubting and perhaps with her second son, the more orthodox James, she became part of the Jewish church in Jerusalem, a mother of Christian believers. This was a more human and likely destiny than the absurd adventures that appeared in apocrypha.

Hans Küng concludes: 'Mary is mother of Jesus. She is a human and not a heavenly being. As a human being and as a mother, she is a witness of his true humanity, but also of his origin from God... Mary is the example and model of Christian faith. Her faith, which feels the sword of scandal, dissension and contradiction, and is required in face of the cross... Hence she was seen later . . . as image and type of the church.'[11]

[11]*ibid.*, p. 459. Compare J. de Satgé, *Mary and the Christian Gospel*, 1976; and contrast, B. Bernard, *The Queen of Heaven*, 1986. See also Uta Ranke-Heinemann, *Eunuchs for the Kingdom of Heaven*, 1991, p. 345: 'Traditional Mariology does not deserve its name. It has become a sort of anti-Mariology, since although it purports to exalt the greatness and dignity of a woman and to paint them in scholarly theological fashion against a gold background, in reality its clumsy fingers crush what constitutes feminine dignity in particular (Mary) and in general (all women).'

14

Joseph

Deprived of his natural function in Matthean and apocryphal legend, Joseph might appear to be almost irrelevant. Yet Jesus is called 'son of Joseph' in the Gospels of Luke and John, and 'son of the carpenter' in Matthew, so that Joseph's parenthood was recognized. Like Mary, Joseph is important still in relationship to the Christ.

Joseph is named seven times in Matthew, seven in Luke, not at all in Mark, and twice in John. He is not mentioned anywhere else in the New Testament.

During the period of the ministry of Jesus the Gospels refer to his mother and brothers and sisters, and the brothers also appear in the early church, in Acts and in some epistles. But Joseph played no part in the development of the church, probably because he was no longer alive.[1]

It may be taken as established that Jesus was Joseph's and Mary's firstborn son, and then they had four other sons and two or more daughters. At one child a year that would mean that Jesus would be seven or eight years old when the last child was born, and the spacing of the offspring may have been greater. If Joseph died when Jesus was in his teens or twenties, then Jesus as eldest son would say the funeral *kaddish* prayers for his father, and then he would act as head of the household. With his mother Mary, Jesus would be responsible for training the younger brothers in trades, and helping to arrange marriages for the sisters. Perhaps that was why Jesus did not begin his public ministry until he was about thirty years of age (Luke 3, 23).

STARTED PREACHING AFTER MET J.B.

---

[1] R. Bauckham, *Jude and the Relatives of Jesus*, p. 6f.

'Joseph was an old man, when he wedded Mary,' said an old English carol, and this notion goes back to Pseudo-James, which had Joseph saying of the proposed guardianship of Mary, 'I am an old man, but she is a girl'. However there is no evidence for this ageing of Joseph in the Bible, and a Roman Catholic writer considers that it is 'unlikely' in view of the duties implied in the bringing up of Jesus and the rest of the family.[2]

* * * * *

It has been assumed, and made popular in Nativity plays, that Joseph was a carpenter. But there is only one Biblical verse where this is suggested (Matthew 13, 55) and this is disputed (see discussion in chapter 4). Some commentators who wish to preserve belief in the Virginal Conception of Jesus, have thought it scandalous that he could have been called 'son of the carpenter and Mary', so they prefer making Jesus himself the carpenter. But there may have been scribal alterations to harmonize the texts of Mark and Matthew, and to some extent of Luke.

Origen, in reply to Celsus, denied that Jesus had been described as an artisan in the Gospels current in the church, for the verse referred to his father, he said. But Justin Martyr, a century or so earlier, wrote of Jesus as having made ploughs and yokes. Even if Jesus was 'the carpenter', there is no reason to suppose that Joseph was not also a carpenter, since trades were passed down in families. Contrariwise, if Joseph was a carpenter, Jesus would probably be one also.

The word 'carpenter' could be used of workers in stone or metal, but most likely in the Gospels it indicates a worker in wood. The apocryphal Gospel of Thomas, which writes of Jesus and 'his father Joseph', says that the latter was a carpenter who made ploughs and yokes. Then a fantasy was added, by stating that when Joseph was asked to make a bed for a rich man the wood was too short, so the child Jesus told his father Joseph to hold one end of the wood while he stretched out the other to the required length.[3]

* * * * *

[2] D. H. Farmer, *The Oxford Dictionary of Saints*, p. 223.
[3] *The Apocryphal New Testament*, p. 52f.

Much more is said in the Gospels of the family of Joseph than that of Mary, since the two genealogies of Matthew and Luke trace his ancestry back to David, Abraham and Adam (see chapter 1). In Matthew's story (1, 20) Joseph is hailed as 'Joseph, son of David', and in Luke (2, 4) he is of 'the house and lineage of David'. It is possible that Joseph and his family may have claimed to be descended from David, even if it was only a lateral branch of the family, and this was later stated by relatives of Jesus in Galilee (see chapters 5 and 8 above).

Joseph's brother seems to have been the Clopas whose wife Mary was at the Cross (John 19, 25), and their son Symeon succeeded to the leadership of the church in Jerusalem, as cousin of Jesus.

The four sons of Joseph, named in the Gospels, are not doubted to have been his own children, and it is natural to assume that they were born of his wife Mary. That they were so clearly named suggests that they were known in the early church.

The daughters of Joseph, at least two, have been named as Mary and Salome, since early centuries. In Pseudo-James, Salome is introduced without explanation, and when she 'made trial', to see if Mary was still a virgin, her hand caught fire, but this was healed when she took the baby into her arms. The assumption was that Salome was an elder child, but this cannot be deduced from the Gospels. A Coptic History of Joseph mentions Salome in the flight into Egypt, but it names the two daughters of Joseph as Lysia and Lydia. None of these identifications are reliable.

* * * * *

Joseph does not figure anywhere during the ministry of Jesus, although his mother and brothers and sisters appear from time to time, as has been noted. There is, however, one other suggestion of reference to Joseph whose significance is often overlooked.

Jesus regularly spoke of God as Father, not Mother. The word *abba* for father has been preserved in his own Aramaic language, notably in the account of Gethsemane (Mark 14, 36) where it evidently impressed the disciples. This use of Abba in prayer has been claimed as peculiar to Jesus, but this is disputed. Certainly God is often called Father in the Bible and ancient Judaism, and his fatherly care for his people was frequently expressed. Jesus was in a long tradition of regarding God as Father, though he did emphasize it.

Some modern translators interpret Abba as 'Dad' or 'Daddy', the language of a child for its father. But this is unlikely and there is no linguistic support for such translation. *Abba* was also used in solemn situations, such as swearing by the life or the head of one's *abba* or father.[4]

What is sure is that Jesus spoke of Father, my Father, our Father, O Father, when referring to God. The common liturgical phrase 'Our Father who art in heaven' does not simply indicate a God in the sky, but it distinguishes the divine Father from the human. Jews were careful to use reverential terms, and they avoided direct mention of the divine name, the tetragrammaton, YHWH. They would never utter the name of Yahweh, in the crude manner of some modern Christian translators, and Jews still substitute Adonai, Lord, for this term. So 'Our Father in heaven' means 'Our Father God', not using the name directly.

The difference between an earthly father and the divine Father is clear. But it is possible, even probable, that Jesus formed some of his conceptions of God from his father Joseph. If he grew up as eldest son, and worked in the carpenter's shop, sharing the work and struggles of a village artisan with a growing family, then his frequent use of Father for God may shed some light on the character and devotion of Joseph too.

Further, Jewish society was patriarchal, and Joseph would have a great influence over Jesus and the other children. In Nazareth, Joseph would not be overshadowed by Mary as he was in later church devotion.

* * * * *

Some Jewish Nazarene or Ebionite Christians continued the Gospel practice and spoke of Jesus as 'born of Joseph and Mary'

[4]G. Vermes, *The Gospel of Jesus the Jew*, p. 27.

(see chapter 10), but as the Gentile churches spread most of them held different views. Joseph was of decreasing interest, his name conserved but his role distorted through his supposed connection with Mary, as a very old man and a pattern of asceticism and holiness.

The cult of Joseph first flourished in Egypt and he came to be especially venerated in the Orthodox East. A *History of Joseph the Carpenter,* or the *Death of Joseph,* was compiled some time between the fourth and seventh centuries. The ideal age for the close of life in Egypt was said to be 110 years, so Joseph was thought to have lived longer, and he became the patron of all who desire a holy death.

This apocryphal work stated that after Joseph's 111th year his death drew near, and he went to the temple and prayed at the altar to be saved from the terrors of death. Back in Nazareth he fell ill and his strength gave way, so that Jesus sat at his head and Mary at his feet. Death and his satellites came to the door armed with fire, but Jesus rebuked them and they fled. Then Jesus told Death to enter and do his appointed work, and Michael and Gabriel put Joseph's soul in a silken napkin and took it away singing. Jesus closed the eyes and mouth of the body and comforted Mary. The apostles asked why Joseph should not have been exempted from death, like Enoch and Elijah, and Jesus replied that they too would still have to die, since death is inevitable for all creatures.[5]

Of course all this is imaginary, but these and similar ideas helped the popularity of Joseph when his cult spread to the West. Many hospitals and churches were dedicated to Joseph, and his name became popular as a Christian name. In a different way, old Joseph was often a figure of fun in medieval mystery plays, depicted as impotent with his virgin wife, to provide comic relief.

Partly in reaction against such lampoons, later medieval leaders propagated devotions to Joseph. In the sixteenth century Teresa of Avila dedicated the mother-house of her reformed convents to Joseph and recommended devotion to him

---

[5]*The Apocryphal New Testament,* p. 84f.

frequently in her writings. The feast of Joseph was celebrated on 19 March, before Lady Day, and his patronage of the universal church on the third Wednesday after Easter. Pius XII in the present century fixed the feast of St Joseph the Worker significantly on May Day, the holiday for working class movements across Europe. The name of Joseph was introduced into the Canon of the Mass by John XXIII in 1962.

In art old Joseph was often represented carrying the child Jesus and holding a lily or staff, symbols perhaps of purity and virility, or age. The church held Joseph to be patron of fathers of families, but this would have been more to the point if Joseph had been frankly recognized as the father of Jesus, with the large family at Nazareth, a full and loving household, where sexual relationships were enjoyed and blessed.

It has been common to write of Joseph as 'foster-father', or 'step-father', or 'legal' father of Jesus; 'father of the historical Jesus', or 'spouse of the BVM'; though nowadays writers from different church traditions may refer to him simply as 'father of Jesus'.

Yet, as it has been seen, from many references in the Gospels, Joseph was the real father of Jesus, and his son receives the honourable title of 'son of Joseph'. For us, Joseph was a carpenter, young and ardent when his family began and in love with Mary. Perhaps he died in his forties or fifties, and thereafter his eldest son shared in the care of the young family with his mother. But the influence of Joseph endured in the understanding of a loving father in the teachings of Jesus.

Since Joseph was the natural father of Jesus, it might be speculated what Jesus would have thought if he had known that down the ages his beloved father, who provided him with a favourite model of the divinity, would have been set aside by his followers and his parenthood denied. What would Mary have thought if she had known that her husband, father of her seven children, would be emasculated and her own maidenhood exaggerated against her maternity? The natural fatherhood of Joseph fits better into the picture of real incarnation, and provides a better moral example, than the artificialities of traditional teachings.

The Man Christ Jesus

The nature of the parentage of Jesus is of great importance for both Christology and moral teaching, which are directly affected by beliefs in the natural or miraculous conception and birth. Theories of the origins of Christ, the relationships of his parents, and the composition of the family at Nazareth, all these have influenced moral concepts of virginity or motherhood and fatherhood, celibacy or marriage, asceticism or sex.

If the Nativity stories of Matthew and Luke are not to be taken as fully factual history, not to mention the wild fantasies of the apocrypha, and if they are partly legendary and speculative, then the human story of Jesus needs restatement in the light of modern critical study.

It seems a fair and reasonable conclusion from the surveys in the previous chapters that, on account of most of the biblical evidence, Jesus was the natural and legitimate son of Joseph and Mary. But such an interpretation appears to go against the doctrines and devotions of the greater part of the church down the ages, which held the logically and biologically impossible views that Mary was a virgin when Jesus was born and remained ever-virgin afterwards. Does it matter?

The Anglican theologian John Macquarrie remarks that belief in the Virginal Conception, 'though it is not found in the earlier witnesses of Paul and Mark, has nevertheless been taken into the fabric of orthodox Christian faith and is affirmed in the catholic creeds. But in spite of the fact that the virginal conception (commonly called the "virgin birth") has the status of a dogma in the church, I think we have to look at this dogma very critically and ask whether it makes any worthwhile theological contribution to christology'.[1]

Not only Paul and Mark, but Hebrews, James, Jude, the latest Gospel John, and apparently all Christian preaching before the appearance of Matthew in the last quarter of the first century, seem to have ignored the notion of a virginal conception. Then for several centuries there were some Christians who held that Joseph was the natural father of Jesus, though they were opposed by those who termed themselves 'orthodox' and 'catholic'.

There are several points at issue, and probably others involved, and something must be said on them. Were most of the church teachers wrong, and could Christianity have continued in error for so long? If it is a divine foundation, the churches have nevertheless proved all too human in the countless quarrels and schisms of their history. No human being or organisation is perfect, and to claim inerrancy for the church is to appropriate what belongs to God and can be construed as blasphemous.

The Eastern and Western churches separated over the Filioque clause in the creed, that the Spirit proceeded from the Father 'and the Son'. The Roman Catholic church diverged from Orthodox and Protestant in asserting as dogmas both the Immaculate Conception and the Assumption of the Virgin Mary. From the first days, and for nearly two thousand years, the church condoned slavery. It has been anti-semitic and viciously persecuting of Jews as God-killers, and Christians are only now recognizing the theological error and moral shame of accusations of Deicide. There has been almost institutionalized misogyny, regarding women as inferior to men or a source of evil, and there has been a generally degrading attitude to sex. Therefore it is possible that the church's central faith and ethic, its Christology and its teaching on sex and the family, have been distorted by erroneous views on the birth of Christ.

* * * * *

[1] *Jesus Christ in Modern Thought*, p. 393.

'There is one God, and there is one mediator between God and men, the man Christ Jesus', says an early confession of faith (1 Timothy 2, 5). The nature and work of Christ were debated backwards and forwards in the churches for centuries, and both 'orthodox' and 'heretic' often went far beyond what could be justified from scripture. Much of the argument relied upon dubious texts, and even more dubious exegesis, and both patristic and apocryphal writings made assumptions that few would accept today. In modern times, to find an acceptable basis for understanding of Christ, the evidence of the Bible must be considered critically.

John Macquarrie continues his discussion by questioning whether belief in a virginal conception makes any worthwhile contribution to Christology, or whether it distorts that doctrine. 'Would the belief that Jesus was born of one human parent alone in any way enhance his stature in our eyes or his authority as one sent by God or the claim that he is the paradigm of humanity? I do not believe so.' On the contrary, such a doctrine encourages the wrong kind of Christology, which remains in some quarters today, and which regards Christ as a sort of 'divine man', different in substance from every other human being, and it 'demeans' him by turning him into a wonder-worker.

Like the Buddha, the Christ has been popularly seen as floating above the ground, or the water, or frozen into a figure from a stained-glass window. In popular Passion Plays, like Oberammergau, not only was there anti-semitism, there was also artificiality in which Christ was stilted and postured (really 'passionless', crucified in a body-stocking!), and only Judas came alive. It is easier to depict a bad man than a good. From his birth to his death the humanity of Jesus was obscured and only now, with scientific study of the Gospels, can it be discovered again.

There is a further loss entailed by the notion of virginal conception, in that any 'imitation of Christ' seems to be impossible, so that his teachings become irrelevant. 'If we suppose Christ to have been conceived and born in an altogether unique way, then it seems that we have separated him from the rest of the human race and thereby made him irrelevant to the human quest for salvation or for the true life. We would be saying not that he is the revelation of God shedding light in our darkness, but that he is an altogether unintelligible anomaly, thrust into the middle of history.'[2]

Many eminent theologians share such a critical view of this tradition. On the Roman Catholic side, Hans Küng writes that 'although the virgin birth cannot be understood as a historical-biological event, it can be regarded as a meaningful *symbol* at least for that time'. Christ was regarded as making a new beginning, a New Covenant, and 'this new beginning then can be proclaimed also *today* without the aid of the legend of the virgin birth, which is more than ever liable to be misunderstood in modern times. No one can be obliged to believe in the biological fact of a virginal conception or birth. Christian faith is related — even without a virgin birth — to the crucified and still living Jesus'.[3]

Such words may bring help to those who seek to understand their faith in the light of modern biblical and scientific knowledge. Yet there are many who are untouched by the difficulties, and who hold to traditional statements and devotions. It is not our purpose to attack or defend them, but to consider the needs of other Christians and would-be believers, and to suggest a defensible apologetic. Protestants and liberal Catholics need not be concerned with polemic, but with arriving at a valid understanding of the accounts of the birth and family of Jesus.

There are very many people who do not know what to think about the Nativity stories, the contradictions and dreamlike character of which are evident, and which may be a hindrance to faith. As one example of many the novelist Susan Hill, a lifelong and profoundly religious person, writes in her moving autobiography, 'In strictly Christian, religious terms, I am never sure what I think about the Christmas story . . . I don't believe it literally, and I don't believe that matters'.[4]

[2]*ibid.*, loc. cit.
[3]*On Being a Christian*, p. 456.
[4]*Family*, 1989, p. 130.

If the laity, and many clergy, are dubious, no alternative is generally offered to them; about the Christmas story, about the humanity of Jesus, about sex and family life. The attitude of church leaders seems to be: 'don't rock the boat', or 'say nothing, for fear of offending the few'. Often indeed the clergy do not know, or do not want to know, what scholars have been writing for many years, and it does not get through to their congregations. And so, 'the hungry sheep look up, and are not fed'.

* * * * *

Statements in the creeds cause difficulties for some worshippers. How can one recite 'conceived by the Holy Ghost, born of the Virgin Mary', if the virginal conception is denied? The use of a creed was originally placed at baptism, confessing the faith at conversion. There was no creed used in the chief western Sunday liturgy for a thousand years, and experts have said that we ought to go back to the older liturgical tradition and not make the creeds a necessary feature of all our services.

Even so, credal statements are symbolical, and the French rightly call a creed a 'symbole'. Creeds are poetry, like hymns, in which many statements are not historical or to be taken literally; they are claims of faith, not facts of history.

Part of the difficulty is our more precise or literal interpretation of history, compared with those of ancient times. Both the evangelists and makers of creeds, remarks R. E. Brown, 'do not dovetail with our modern questions of historicity and dogmatic significance, and what are problems to us often were not problems to them'. The expansion of old baptismal confessions of faith into creeds with reference both to the birth and the death of Christ was 'at least in part, to counter a heresy that questioned the reality of Jesus' humanity'.[5]

In fact it may be claimed that the creeds do not go far enough. They show a strong interest in the pre-existence of Christ and in his post-existence, but of his earthly career they

[5]*The Birth of the Messiah*, p. 517f.

say next to nothing, save that he was born and died. They have
been said to provide a 'three days' Christology, instead of
'thirty years'.[6] Whether it is the Apostles' or the Nicene Creed,
we are taken direct from the birth to the death of Christ, with
nothing on his life and teaching, his value and example, which
modern Christians consider to be of supreme importance.

* * * * *

One major gain in holding to the fatherhood of Joseph and the
natural birth of Jesus, is that they allow for a better understanding
of the humanity of Christ than has been possible since the first
days of the Gospel. It may seem strange to think that the
twentieth century can understand the first century more than
was done in the intervening eras, but that is just what critical
textual and historical study can provide. By cutting through the
legendary accretions, the fantasies of apocryphas, and the false
emphases of cults, and comparing and assessing the Gospel
accounts, at least the outlines of the story become clearer. It is
probable that nowadays both Christians and non-Christians
think more of Jesus as a man than was possible in earlier
centuries, and for the Christian a viable Christology must begin
from the humanity.

There is an understandable reluctance on the part of leaders
and ordinary Christians to be negative, to deny the Virgin Birth
without putting anything in its place. But positive statements
can be made, and they should be declared more clearly and
publicly. If Joseph was the father of Jesus, that should be
affirmed and shown to be an integral part of the humanity of
the Christ, with all the advantages to understanding that it can
bring. But where are the writings and speakers who admit and
state this?

It is remarkable that one of the few declarations of 'Jesus, son
of Joseph' should come from an eminent and sympathetic
Jewish scholar. Dr Geza Vermes states 'the case for natural
paternity, one (negative) argument in favour of it is that Mark

---

[6]A. Wessels, *Images of Jesus*, p. 179; and see P. Lapide and J. Moltmann, *Jewish Monotheism and Christian Trinitarian Doctrine*, 1981.

makes no mention of an alternative. In addition, Matthew and
Luke allude in their main story to the "father of Jesus" as
though having forgotten the supernatural agency described in
their infancy stories. Secondly, the logic of the genealogies
demands that Joseph was the father of Jesus'.[7]

* * * * *

In addition to its damaging effects upon Christological
teachings, the doctrine of the Virginal Conception is
unsatisfactory and injurious on ethical grounds. It denies the
paternity of Joseph, it forbids full married life and sexual
relationships in the Holy Family, at least in the developed
notions of the Virgin Birth. Continued motherhood is denied
to Mary, female virginity is exalted above maternity, and male
virginity is often implied also, and support is given for the
claims of the superiority of celibacy to marriage.

The Virginal Conception is stated probably only clearly by
Matthew, and all his Nativity stories are dominated by a
determination to create fulfilments of prophecy, which
nowadays are seen as unconvincing. Even Matthew, however,
only sees a power of a holy spirit, not a depreciation of natural
procreation. It must be repeated that there is no suggestion in
Matthew's or Luke's accounts that normal sexual relations
between Joseph and Mary would have been unclean or unworthy
of the Messiah, and no hint of belief in Original Sin. But the
defiling nature of the sexual act came to be held by the church,
and the role of sex in the transmission of Original Sin was
expressed as late as the nineteenth century in the Roman
Catholic dogma of the Immaculate Conception.

The work of celibate theologians in formulating distortions
of attitudes to sex and marriage can hardly be over-estimated.
A similar process can be observed in Buddhist stories, also
compiled by celibate monks, first of the miraculous and then of
the virginal conception of the Buddha.

In the Christian world, especially among the celibate clergy
of the West, along with notions of the evil concupiscence of sex,

[7] *Jesus the Jew*, p. 215.

there went the views, from Augustine to Aquinas and beyond, that women were inferior to men in all respects, with the single exception of child-bearing.[8]

From the general Biblical picture, however, the blessings of marriage and sexual relationships are abundantly clear. In the myths of creation it was said that a man 'cleaves to his wife, and they become one flesh'. God created them 'in his own image', 'male and female he created them', and he told them to 'be fruitful and multiply' (Genesis 2, 24; 1, 27-28).

Jesus himself blessed marriage, confirming the divine institution of Genesis and adding 'so they are no longer two but one flesh' (Mark 10, 8). The general Biblical emphasis is upon the sanctity of marriage, and the procreative process which followed naturally, and never on their denial in ascetic notions of unconsummated marriage.

In these days of confusion in sexual and marital matters, it is essential to point to the Christian ideal and to see it demonstrated in the family of Christ. There are those who are natural celibates or homosexuals; 'there are some who have been eunuchs from birth', and some 'have made themselves eunuchs for the sake of the kingdom of heaven' (Matthew 19, 12). But the great majority are not so, and marriage and the family are their goal.

If there was a natural conception and birth of Jesus, then Joseph and Mary can be understood better than in the past. They can be pictured with their large family, and the joys and cares of that family itself can be appreciated. In theological terms 'the man Christ Jesus' can be understood and followed more clearly in this rich context. There are also ethical models of normal and rightful sexual relations, of marriage and family, of parenthood and brotherly and sisterly affection.

To conclude: Joseph was the father of Jesus, Mary was Joseph's wife in the fullest sense, and the family at Nazareth completed the picture. Christmas and the Nativity are about the family, and they can be freed from fantasies that mislead in both theology and devotion.

[8] *Sex in the World's Religions*, p. 222ff.

Index

HERESIES – p. 77
WOMEN – p. 107